AF429440

Brinji Rice

Veg brinji is a delicious one pot dish made with spices, coconut milk, rice and mixed veggies. The recipe comes from Tamil Nadu.

Prep Time   :   10 mins

Cook Time   :   20 mins

Total Time   :   30 mins

Cuisine   :   South Indian, Tamil Nadu

Servings   :   4

<u>Ingredients</u>

<u>for soaking rice</u>

1.5 cups basmati rice

enough water for soaking rice

<u>for ground masala paste</u>

3 tablespoons chopped coriander leaves

3 tablespoons chopped mint leaves

2 to 3 green chilies - chopped

2 inch ginger or 2 teaspoons chopped ginger

6 to 7 medium garlic cloves or 2 teaspoons chopped garlic

1 tablespoon grated coconut

1 inch cinnamon

2 cloves

2 green cardamoms

½ teaspoon fennel seeds

4 to 5 tablespoons water or add as required

other ingredients for brinji rice

3 tablespoons oil

1 inch cinnamon

2 cloves

1 green cardamoms

1 large tej patta or 2 to 3 medium to small tej patta (birinj elai or indian bay leaf)

½ cup sliced onions or 1 medium onion, thinly sliced

⅓ cup chopped tomatoes or 1 medium tomato, chopped

½ to ¾ cup chopped cauliflower florets

½ cup chopped carrots

½ cup chopped potato

⅓ cup chopped capsicum

⅓ cup green peas - fresh or frozen

¼ cup chopped french beans

2 cups coconut milk

½ cup water

salt as required

Instructions

for soaking rice

Rinse 1.5 cups of basmati rice very well in water till the water runs clear of starch. Then soak rice in enough water for 30 minutes.

After 30 minutes, drain all the water and keep aside.

preparation for brinji rice

In a small grinder jar take chopped coriander leaves, chopped mint leaves, green chilies, chopped ginger, chopped garlic and grated coconut.

Add 1 inch cinnamon, 2 cloves, 2 green cardamoms and ½ teaspoon fennel seeds (saunf).

Add 4 to 5 tablespoons of water and grind to a smooth masala paste. Keep aside.

making brinji rice

Heat 3 tablespoons oil in a 3 litre pressure cooker. You can also use ghee instead of oil. Add 1 large tej patta or 2 to 3 medium to small tej patta (birinj elai).

Immediately add 1 inch cinnamon, 2 cloves and 1 green cardamom.

Fry spices for a few seconds till they become aromatic.

Then add ½ cup sliced onions. Stir and mix.

Stirring often, sauté onions till they turn translucent or light brown.

Then add ⅓ cup chopped tomatoes. mix well and begin to sauté tomatoes on medium-low flame till they soften.

Now add the ground masala paste. mix very well and begin to sauté masala on a low flame till you see oil releasing from the sides of the masala paste.

Then add the veggies. mix very well and sauté for a minute.

Then add the rice. gently mix rice grains with the veggies.

Now add 2 cups coconut milk.

Add ½ cup of water. If you use very thick coconut milk, then add ¾ cup water.

Season with salt as required. stir and mix well. Check the taste of water and it should be slightly salty. If not, then add some more salt.

Pressure cook on medium flame for 8 minutes or 1 to 2 whistles. when pressure drops down on its own, open the lid of the cooker.

Gently fluff the rice and mix so that the top coconut milk layer gets mixed evenly with the bottom rice layer. Mix gently and do not over do.

Serve veg brinji rice with any raita.

Kuska Recipe

Kuska rice is South Indian style spiced flavorful biryani rice served as an accompaniment with a gravy dish.

Prep Time   :   30 mins

Cook Time   :   15 mins

Total Time   :   45 mins

Cuisine   :   South Indian

Servings   :   2 to 3

Ingredients

main ingredients

1 cup heaped basmati rice or 215 grams basmati rice

2 tablespoons ghee

50 grams onions or 1 medium onion or ⅓ cup thinly sliced onions

65 grams tomato or 1 medium to large tomato or ½ cup chopped tomatoes

1 teaspoon Ginger-Garlic Paste

1 or 2 green chilies - sliced or slit

½ tablespoon chopped mint leaves

2 tablespoons chopped coriander leaves

2 cups water or 2.25 cups water

1 teaspoon lemon juice

salt as required

few coriander leaves or mint leaves for garnish

whole spices

½ teaspoon shah jeera

1 inch cinnamon

2 to 3 cloves

2 green cardamoms

1 to 2 single strands of mace

1 tej patta (indian bay leaf)

Instructions

soaking rice

Rinse 1 cup heaped basmati rice (215 grams) very well in water till the water runs clear of starch. Soak rice in enough water for 30 minutes. Later drain all the water and keep the rice aside.

making kuska rice

Heat 2 tablespoons ghee in a pot or pan.

Add the following spices and let them splutter - 1/2 teaspoon caraway seeds (shah jeera), 1 inch cinnamon, 2 to 3 cloves, 2 green cardamoms, 1 to 2 single strands of mace and 1 tej patta.

Then add 1/3 cup thinly sliced onions.

Saute the onions on a low to medium flame stirring often, till they start turning light golden.

Then add 1 teaspoon ginger-garlic paste.

Stir and saute on a low flame till the raw aroma of ginger and garlic goes away.

Add 1/2 cup chopped tomatoes and saute for a minute. You can even skip tomatoes if you want.

Then add 1 or 2 green chilies (sliced or slit), 1/2 tablespoon chopped mint leaves and 2 tablespoons chopped coriander leaves. Mix very well.

Now add 2 cups of water. Instead of water you can also use veg stock. Depending on the quality of rice, you can add 2 to 2.25 cups of water.

cooking kuska rice

Cover the pan with its lid.

On a medium flame, bring the entire water mixture to a boil.

When the water starts boiling, then add the rice.

Season with salt as per taste and mix very well. Check the taste of the water and it should taste a bit salty. If not, then add some more salt.

Add 1 teaspoon lemon juice. Again stir.

Place a cotton kitchen towel or napkin on the pan. You can also seal the pan with an aluminium foil. Now place the lid on the pan.

Keep the flame to a low or sim and dum cook till the rice grains are tender and cooked. It will take about 7 to 8 minutes for the rice to cook. Do use a thick bottomed pan, so that the rice grains do not stick to the bottom of the pan. If you want you can check the rice grains once while cooking. If all the water has been absorbed and the rice grains do not look cooked, then add some hot water in the pan. Cover and continue to cook.

When the rice grains are cooked, then allow resting time of 5 to 7 minutes.

Then gently fluff the rice with a fork.

Serve kuska rice garnished with a few coriander or mint leaves along with a veg gravy or dal of your choice.

Notes

- you can also use seeraga samba rice instead of basmati rice.

Veg Biryani (Hyderabadi Vegetable Dum Biryani)

A vegetable biryani recipe from the land of the nawabs - Hyderabad. The Hyderabadi vegetable biryani recipe is light, a bit spiced, aromatic and deliciously yum.

Prep Time   : 45 mins

Cook Time : 45 mins

Total Time   : 1 hr 30 mins

Cuisine   : Hyderabadi, Indian

Servings   : 5

Ingredients

For soaking rice

1.5 cups basmati rice - 300 grams, preferably aged basmati rice

1 cup water for soaking rice

veggies

1.5 cups cauliflower florets - 150 grams

1 cup chopped potatoes - 100 grams or 2 medium-sized

½ cup chopped carrots - 100 grams or 1 medium to large carrot

¼ cup chopped french beans - 50 grams or 11 to 12 french beans

8 to 10 white button mushrooms, sliced or chopped, (optional)

¼ to ⅓ cup chopped bell pepper - 50 grams or 1 small to medium (optional)

½ cup green peas - fresh or frozen

1 cup thinly sliced onions (heaped) - 115 grams onion or 1 large onion

1.5 tablespoons finely chopped ginger - 10 grams or 2 pieces of 2 inch ginger or 1 tablespoon ginger paste

1 tablespoon finely chopped garlic - 5 grams or 10 to 12 medium garlic cloves or ½ tablespoon garlic paste

2 green chilies - slit or sliced

For cooking rice

3 green cardamoms

1 black cardamom

3 cloves

1 inch cinnamon

1 tej patta (indian bay leaf)

2 single mace strands

5 cups water

½ teaspoon salt or add as per taste

For biryani curry/gravy

3 tablespoons ghee (clarified butter) - use 3 tablespoons oil instead

1 teaspoon shah jeera (caraway seeds)

1 tej patta (indian bay leaf)

3 green cardamoms

1 black cardamom

1 inch cinnamon

1 cup Curd (yogurt), whisked - 200 grams

½ teaspoon turmeric powder

1 teaspoon red chilli powder or cayenne pepper or paprika

½ cup water for pressure cooking and ¾ cup water if cooking in a pot

2 tablespoons cashews

1 tablespoons raisins or sultanas (without seeds)

2 tablespoons almonds - raw or blanched, peeled and sliced

salt as required

For assembling and layering

⅓ cup chopped coriander leaves (cilantro) - 20 grams

⅓ cup chopped mint leaves - 5 grams

4 to 5 tablespoons milk

¼ teaspoon saffron strands

2 teaspoons kewra water (pandanus water) or rose water

Instructions

Preparation

Pick and rinse basmati rice in running water till the water runs clear of starch. Soak the rice in 1 cup of water for 30 minutes.

After 30 minutes drain the rice and keep aside.

When the rice is soaking, prep all the veggies and other ingredients. Keep aside.

Cooking rice

Take a deep bottomed pan. Add water and heat the water on a high flame.

When the water becomes hot, add all the salt and following spices: tej patta, green cardamoms, cloves, black cardamom, cinnamon, strands of mace.

Bring the water to a boil. Then add the rice.

Just gently stir with a spoon or fork, after you add the rice.

Do not reduce the flame and continue to cook the rice.

The rice has to be ¾th cooked. The grains should have a slight bite to them when cooked. The rice should not be fully cooked but almost cooked.

Drain the rice in a colander. Gently fluff and keep aside.

Making vegetable curry/gravy

In a pressure cooker or a pan, heat ghee. Add the following spices - shah jeera, tej patta, green cardamoms, cloves, black cardamom and cinnamon. Sauté the whole spices till they crackle.

Now add the onions. Stir and sauté them on a low to medium flame.

Add a pinch of salt to quicken the cooking process.

When the onions are cooking, take 1 cup fresh curd (yogurt) in a bowl and whisk the curd with a spoon or wired whisk till it becomes smooth.

Sauté the onions till they become golden brown or caramelize.

Then add the ginger-garlic paste and sliced green chillies. You can also finely chop the ginger-garlic and add.

Sauté till the raw aroma of ginger-garlic goes away.

Add the turmeric and red chili powder. Stir and mix well.

Next add the chopped veggies. Sauté for a minute or two.

Lower the heat and add the whisked curd (yogurt). Stir and mix well as soon as you add the curd. Then add water.

Season with salt. Stir again.

Pressure cook for 1 whistle on medium flame. If cooking in a pot, then cook till the vegetables are done. Don't over cook the vegetables.

Warm 4 to 5 tablespoons milk in a microwave or in a small pan on the stove top. Add ¼ teaspoon of saffron strands. Stir and keep aside.

When the pressure settles down on its own, remove the lid and check the gravy. If the vegetables are not cooked well, then keep the cooker on the stove top and simmer the vegetable biryani gravy without the lid, till the vegetables are cooked. If there is too much water or stock in the gravy, then simmer till some water dries up. The veg biryani gravy should have a medium or slightly thick consistency and should not be watery.

Now add cashews, raisins and almonds (blanched or raw) to the vegetable gravy. Mix and stir. Keep aside. Do check the salt. Add more if required.

Assembling & layering

Now in a thick bottomed pan, layer half of the veg biryani gravy first.

Then layer half of the rice.

Sprinkle half of the chopped coriander leaves (cilantro), mint leaves and saffron milk.

Layer the remaining veg biryani gravy.

Layer the remainder of the rice. Sprinkle the remaining coriander leaves, mint leaves, saffron milk on the top. Sprinkle the rose water or kewra water. You can make 2 layers or 4 layers like I have done. But do note that rice should be the last layer.

Dum cooking biryani

Now seal and secure the pot with aluminium foil. Then cover with a lid. You can also seal the handi with a moist cotton cloth and then cover with the lid.

Take a tava/griddle/skillet and heat it on medium flame.

When the tawa becomes hot, lower the flame. Keep the sealed veg biryani handi on the tava. Keep the flame to the lowest and cook for 25 to 30 minutes. You can also dum cook veg biryani for the first 15 minutes on direct low flame and then for the last 10 minutes, place the handi on the hot tawa/skillet and cook on a low flame.

Once done using a fork or spoon check the bottom layer of the biryani. There should be no liquids at the bottom. If there are liquids, then continue to dum cook for some more time. After dum cooking, give a standing time of 5 to 7 minutes and then serve the dum biryani.

Serving Biryani

While serving, make sure you equally serve the vegetables as well as rice.

Serve the delicious hyderabadi veg biryani with your choice of raita, onion salad, mango pickle, roasted papad. Other accompaniments for this biryani are mirchi ka salan and veg shorba gravy.

Notes

For baking veg biryani

You could also preheat the oven to 180 degree Celsius/356 degrees Fahrenheit and then bake the veg biryani in the oven for 30-35 minutes.

Please remember to use an oven proof glass utensil like the pyrex bowl for baking in the oven.

You will have to assemble the vegetable biryani as mentioned above in the ovenproof utensil and then bake it.

Tips

Ingredients: Do try to use all the ingredients as mentioned in the recipe.

Rice: Use a good quality basmati rice – preferably aged basmati rice. You can even use Sella Basmati Rice which is parboiled basmati rice (known as sella basmati rice in Hindi and converted basmati rice outside India). For sella basmati rice, you will need to soak the rice grains for an hour. The cooking time will also increase for this variety of basmati rice.

Cooking of rice: Cook the rice grains till they are ¾th done. They will have a slight bite to them and will be slightly undercooked. Do not cook the rice all the way as they will become mushy by the time the biryani is dum cooked.

Spices: The lovely fragrance and aroma in a biryani comes from using whole spices. Thus the spices need to be fresh and in their shelf life.

Curd (Yogurt): Use fresh yogurt that is slightly sweet and not sour. The curd or yogurt should also be made from whole milk. Do not use fat-free yogurt or curd made from toned milk as it will split while cooking.

Biryani gravy: The curry or gravy for the biryani should have a medium to medium-thick consistency. It should not be watery like a stock or broth as this will lead to the rice becoming mushy or very soft after dum cooking.

Vegan variation: Use almond milk yogurt or cashew milk yogurt. Replace ghee (clarified butter) with oil. You could use any vegetable oil or neutral tasting oil.

Serving Suggestions: Biryani is usually accompanied with a raita (yogurt dip). The raita can be a simple onion raita or made with a mix of onion, tomatoes and cucumber. In Hyderabad, biryani is served with mirchi ka salan (green chilli curry) and raita. You can even serve biryani with a soupy gravy known as shorba gravy.

Peanut Rice

Peanut rice is a tasty South Indian rice variety made with roasted peanut powder, lentils and spices.

Prep Time   :   25 mins

Cook Time   :   5 mins

Total Time   :   30 mins

Cuisine   :   South Indian, Tamil Nadu

Servings   :   4

Ingredients

for cooking rice

1 cup rice

1.75 to 2 cups water or add as required

½ teaspoon salt or add as required

for peanut powder or verkadalai podi

½ cup peanuts

1 tablespoon chana dal (split and husked bengal gram)

1 tablespoon urad dal (split and husked black gram)

3 dry red chilies - broken and seeds removed (can use byadagi or kashmiri red chilies)

3 tablespoons desiccated coconut

¼ teaspoon turmeric powder

1 tablespoon white sesame seeds - optional

for tempering peanut rice

1 tablespoon sesame oil (gingelly oil)

½ teaspoon mustard seeds

8 to 10 curry leaves

1 pinch asafoetida

other ingredient

salt as required, to be added later

Instructions

<u>**cooking rice**</u>

Rinse 1 cup rice a couple of times in water and then soak in enough water for 20 to 30 minutes. If using brown rice, then for about 30 to 45 minutes.

Later drain all the water and add the rice in a pressure cooker. Also add ½ teaspoon salt or add as required.

Add 1.75 to 2 cups water or add as required for regular white rice. If using hand pounded rice then add 2.25 to 2.5 cups water. If using brown rice, then add 3 cups of water.

For white rice, pressure cook for 2 whistles on medium flame. For hand pounded rice, pressure cook for 7 to 8 whistles and for brown rice pressure cook for 10 to 12 whistles on medium flame.

When the pressure settles down on its own, remove the lid.

Take the rice in a large bowl or plate and let the rice grains cool down completely. If there are lumps in the rice, then break the lumps.

<u>**making peanut rice**</u>

Heat a small pan. Keep the flame to a medium-low. Add ½ cup peanuts.

Stirring often begins to roast the peanuts.

Roast till the peanuts become crunchy and crisp. You will see some blisters and black spots on the peanuts.

Remove the roasted peanuts in a plate and keep aside.

In the same pan, then add 1 tablespoon chana dal.

Stirring continuously roast chana dal on a low flame till they change color and become golden. They will also become aromatic. remove and keep aside.

In the same pan add 1 tablespoon urad dal.

Stirring continuously roast urad dal on a low flame till the lentils become golden and aromatic.

Keeping the flame to a low, add 3 dry red chilies and 3 tablespoons desiccated coconut.

Mix and continue to roast stirring continuously.

Roast coconut till it is light golden.

Now switch off flame and add ¼ teaspoon turmeric powder and 1 tablespoon white sesame seeds. Sesame seeds can be skipped.

Mix well. Keep this mixture in the pan till it cools down.

Take the above spices and coconut mixture in a small grinder jar. Also add roasted chana dal.

Grind in small seconds to a coarse mixture. You can even use the pulse option of the mixer-grinder and pulse at intervals of 3 to 4 seconds.

Then add the roasted peanuts.

Using the pulse option for some seconds, grind to a semi fine powder. Do not grind too much as then peanuts will release their oil.

Add the ground peanut powder to the cooked rice. add more salt as per taste and mix very well.

making tempering for peanut rice

Heat 1 tablespoon sesame oil (gingelly oil) in a small pan. Add ½ teaspoon mustard seeds.

Let them crackle.

When the mustard seeds crackle, then add 8 to 10 curry leaves and 1 pinch of asafoetida (hing). Switch off the flame and stir.

Add all the tempered ingredients in the peanut rice mixture. mix again.

Serve peanut rice as a main course or as a side dish.

Notes

Recipe can be halved or doubled or tripled.

Use red chilies which are not very hot or pungent.

For spicy peanut rice, you can add 4 to 5 byadagi or kashmiri red chilies.

For more flavor of sesame seeds, you can add 2 to 3 tablespoons.

You can also use leftover rice.

If you want some chunkiness and crunchiness, then coarsely grind the peanuts.

Pulao Recipe | Veg Pulao

Trying to get more vegetables in your diet? Try this vegetarian one pot meal of pulao. Use the vegetables that you like most, like peas, potatoes, and green beans. Make this simple veg pulao that packs a punch of flavor!

Prep Time   : 15 mins

Cook Time : 25 mins

Total Time :   40 mins

Cuisine   : Indian

Servings   : 4

Ingredients

For soaking rice

1.5 cups basmati rice - 300 grams, rinsed & soaked for 30 minutes

water - as required for soaking

Vegetables

½ to ¾ cup chopped cauliflower florets

½ to ¾ cup chopped potatoes

¼ cup chopped carrots

⅓ cup green peas - fresh or frozen

¼ cup chopped green peas (french beans)

¼ cup chopped green bell pepper (capsicum) - optional

¼ cup sliced baby corn - optional

<u>Other ingredients</u>

3 tablespoons ghee or oil

1 cup thinly sliced onions or 1 large onion, sliced

½ cup chopped tomatoes or 1 medium sized tomato, chopped

1 to 1.5 inches ginger - crushed to a paste in a mortar-pestle

4 to 5 small to medium garlic cloves

1 to 2 green chillies (chili pepper)

3 tablespoons chopped coriander leaves (cilantro)

2 tablespoons chopped mint leaves - optional

¼ teaspoon lemon juice - optional

2.5 to 3 cups water or veg stock * check notes below for details. I added 3 cups of water

salt as required

<u>Whole spices</u>

1 teaspoon cumin seeds or 1 teaspoon caraway seeds (shah jeera)

5 to 6 whole black pepper - optional

1 tej patta (indian bay leaf)

4 cloves

3 to 4 green cardamoms

1 black cardamom - optional

1 small piece of mace - optional

1 small star anise - optional

1 inch cinnamon

1 small piece of stone flower (dagad phool aur patthar ke phool) - optional

<u>For garnish</u>

1 to 2 tablespoons chopped coriander leaves or mint leaves

<u>Instructions</u>

<u>Preparation</u>

Rinse rice till the water runs clear of starch and become transparent while rinsing.

Soak the rice in enough water for 30 minutes. Drain all the water and keep the soaked rice aside.

Rinse, peel and chop the vegetables.

Crush chopped ginger, garlic and green chillies to a paste in a mortar-pestle or grind them in a small mixer or grinder with a bit of water.

<u>Frying spices and onions</u>

In a deep thick bottomed pot or pan, heat ghee or oil and fry all the whole spices mentioned above, till the oil becomes fragrant and the spices splutter.

Add the onions and saute them till golden. Saute the onions on a low to medium-low flame and stir often for uniform browning.

Add the ginger-garlic-green chili paste and saute for some seconds till their raw aroma goes away.

Add the tomatoes and saute for 2 to 3 minutes on a low to medium-low flame.

Add all the chopped veggies and saute again for 1 to 2 minutes on a low to medium-low flame.

Add rice and saute gently for 1 to 2 minutes on a low or medium-low flame, so that the rice gets well coated with the oil.

Add water and lemon juice. Mix and stir.

Season with salt and stir again.

Cooking veg pulao

Cover tightly and let the rice cook on a low flame, till the water is absorbed and the rice is well cooked.

Check in between a few times to check if the water is enough. Depending on the quality of rice, you may need to add less or more water. With a fork too, you can gently stir the rice without breaking the rice grains.

Once the rice grains are cooked, fluff and let the rice stand for 5 minutes.

Serve pulao hot with some side salad, sliced onion & lemon wedges or raita. You can also garnish it with chopped coriander or mint leaves or fried cashews or fried onions.

Notes

Tips & Suggestions

Type and quality of rice: Pulao is always made with Basmati rice. The basmati rice should be fragrant and long-grained to get good results. Aged basmati rice will give you the best results. Even parboiled basmati rice (sella basmati) can be used. You can also use other types of long-grained rice and short-grained rice. These Indian rice varieties can be easily purchased from Amazon.

For separate rice grains: Follow these steps to ensure you have separate rice grains in your pulao:

Soak the rice: It is always better to soak your rice for 20 to 30 minutes before cooking. Soaking rice grains gives them a better texture when they are cooked. If you do not have time to soak them, then just rinse the rice before adding it. Note that if you only rinse the rice, you will need to add some more water as pre soaked rice grains require less water for cooking as compared to rice grains which are not soaked.

Add just enough water: Be sure that you do not add too much water, especially if you have presoaked your rice as recommended above.

Sauté the rice: After adding the rice grains to your pan, sauté them for 1 to 2 minutes on a low to medium flame, so that they are coated with fat (oil or ghee). The rice grains have to be separate & and yet well cooked in a pulao or biryani. Adding lemon juice also helps make the rice grains fluffier.

Rice to water ratio: For most rice varieties, the rice to water ratio is generally 1:2. However, this ratio can vary depending on the particular type of rice used or the cooking method used:

Example 1– organic basmati rice requires more water while cooking and parboiled basmati rice will need more water as compared to regular basmati rice. For this reason, I recommend when cooking pulao, to use rice which you have cooked before. This way you will already know how much water to add.

Example 2– when cooking pulao in a pressure cooker, generally less water is added. The steam generated in the cooker helps in cooking the rice grains. However, the amount of water to be added will depend upon the size of the cooker. For example, in larger cookers, more water has to be added.

Vegetables: You can add your favorite vegetables. Note that the vegetables add a lot of flavor to the rice. You can even add mushrooms to give a meaty texture and umami flavor to the pulao. Button Mushrooms, morel mushrooms, cremini mushrooms, shiitake mushrooms can be added.

Fried Rice Recipe

This classic Chinese fried rice recipe is loaded with fresh mixed veggies and aromatic spices for an incredibly hearty, flavorful vegan veg fried rice.

Prep Time   : 15 mins

Cook Time   : 30 mins

Total Time   : 45 min

Cuisine   : Chinese, Indo Chinese

Servings   : 3

Ingredients

For cooking rice

1 cup basmati rice or long grained rice - 190 to 200 grams

4 to 4.5 cups water

½ teaspoon salt or add as required

2 to 3 drops toasted sesame oil or any neutral oil

Other ingredients

3 tablespoons toasted sesame oil or any neutral oil

1 star anise

¾ to 1 teaspoon finely chopped garlic or 3 to 4 small to medium garlic cloves

½ teaspoon finely chopped ginger or ½ inch ginger - optional

¼ cup chopped spring onion whites (scallions)

¼ cup finely chopped french beans

¼ cup finely chopped carrots

¼ to ½ cup finely chopped cabbage - optional

¼ cup chopped bell pepper or capsicum - red, green or yellow

1 cup chopped button mushrooms

1 tablespoon finely chopped celery - skip if you do not have

3 tablespoons soy sauce (naturally brewed) or tamari - can add as required

1 teaspoon rice wine or rice vinegar

½ teaspoon black pepper powder or add as required

2 tablespoons chopped spring onions greens

salt as required

Instructions

Cooking rice

Rinse rice very well till the water runs clear of starch. Soak rice in water for 30 mins. Drain and keep aside.

In a pot, bring water to a gentle boil with salt and 2 to 3 drops of toasted sesame oil.

Add the soaked and drained rice to the hot water.

On a low to medium to medium-high heat simmer rice without the lid.

When rice becomes al dente or just about cooked, remove the pot from the heat. Strain the rice in a colander or sieve.

You can also gently rinse cooked rice in water so that they stop cooking and don't stick to each other. Cover the cooked rice and set aside until the rice cools completely. You can even refrigerate rice with a covered lid for 30 minutes.

Chopping veggies

When the cooked rice is cooling, chop the veggies finely and keep aside.

Remember to chop the french beans very finely. They take more time to cook than other veggies. You can also blanch them first and then cook. Another option is to add the beans first and then add the other vegetables.

Making fried rice

Heat oil in a wok or a pan. First add the star anise and fry for a few seconds or until the oil becomes fragrant.

Add the garlic, ginger and sauté for some seconds. No need to brown the garlic.

Add the spring onions whites and sauté for about 2 minutes.

Then add finely chopped french beans.

Stir fry french beans for 2 to 3 minutes over medium to medium-high heat.

Add the remaining finely chopped veggies, including mushrooms and celery. Increase the heat to a high to thoroughly cook all of the vegetables.

You have to continuously toss and stir while frying so that the veggies are uniformly cooked and do not get burnt.

The vegetables have to be stir-fried, until they are almost cooked and yet retain their crunchiness and crispiness. Stir-frying vegetables on high heat takes about 4 to 6 minutes.

Add the soy sauce, salt and pepper. Stir quickly and add cooked and cooled rice. Stir fry for a few minutes until the sauce has coated the rice well. Keep a check when adding salt, as soy sauce already has salt in it.

Serve the fried rice hot as it is or with your favorite Chinese side.

Serving suggestions

Though fried rice tastes great on its own, you can pair it with Veg Manchurian, Gobi Manchurian, Chilli Paneer, Spring Rolls or Chilli Mushroom. More side recipes for veg fried rice are linked and listed in the main post.

Storing fried rice

Vegetable fried rice stays good for a couple of days. But I would recommend it to be eaten as soon as you can since many days old rice is not good for health.

Notes

Ingredient Notes

Rice: Aged, long-grained, non-sticky white rice is the best to make fried rice. Here I have used basmati rice.

Veggies: You can add your favorite vegetables or mushrooms in a total quantity of 1.5 to 2 cups finely chopped mixed vegetables excluding mushrooms. You can vary the amount of each veggie as you like.

Protein: Include tofu, seitan, tempeh, or for a vegetarian option, add paneer.

Fried Rice Recipe

This classic Chinese fried rice recipe is loaded with fresh mixed veggies and aromatic spices for an incredibly hearty, flavorful vegan veg fried rice.

Prep Time   : 15 mins

Cook Time   :   30 mins

Total Time   :   45 min

Cuisine   : Chinese, Indo Chinese

Servings   : 3

Ingredients

For cooking rice

1 cup basmati rice or long grained rice - 190 to 200 grams

4 to 4.5 cups water

½ teaspoon salt or add as required

2 to 3 drops toasted sesame oil or any neutral oil

Other ingredients

3 tablespoons toasted sesame oil or any neutral oil

1 star anise

¾ to 1 teaspoon finely chopped garlic or 3 to 4 small to medium garlic cloves

½ teaspoon finely chopped ginger or ½ inch ginger - optional

¼ cup chopped spring onion whites (scallions)

¼ cup finely chopped french beans

¼ cup finely chopped carrots

¼ to ½ cup finely chopped cabbage - optional

¼ cup chopped bell pepper or capsicum - red, green or yellow

1 cup chopped button mushrooms

1 tablespoon finely chopped celery - skip if you do not have

3 tablespoons soy sauce (naturally brewed) or tamari - can add as required

1 teaspoon rice wine or rice vinegar

½ teaspoon black pepper powder or add as required

2 tablespoons chopped spring onions greens

salt as required

Instructions

Cooking rice

Rinse rice very well till the water runs clear of starch. Soak rice in water for 30 mins. Drain and keep aside.

In a pot, bring water to a gentle boil with salt and 2 to 3 drops of toasted sesame oil.

Add the soaked and drained rice to the hot water.

On a low to medium to medium-high heat simmer rice without the lid.

When rice becomes al dente or just about cooked, remove the pot from the heat. Strain the rice in a colander or sieve.

You can also gently rinse cooked rice in water so that they stop cooking and don't stick to each other. Cover the cooked rice and set aside until the rice cools completely. You can even refrigerate rice with a covered lid for 30 minutes.

Chopping veggies

When the cooked rice is cooling, chop the veggies finely and keep aside.

Remember to chop the french beans very finely. They take more time to cook than other veggies. You can also blanch them first and then cook. Another option is to add the beans first and then add the other vegetables.

Making fried rice

Heat oil in a wok or a pan. First add the star anise and fry for a few seconds or until the oil becomes fragrant.

Add the garlic, ginger and sauté for some seconds. No need to brown the garlic.

Add the spring onions whites and sauté for about 2 minutes.

Then add finely chopped french beans.

Stir fry french beans for 2 to 3 minutes over medium to medium-high heat.

Add the remaining finely chopped veggies, including mushrooms and celery. Increase the heat to a high to thoroughly cook all of the vegetables.

You have to continuously toss and stir while frying so that the veggies are uniformly cooked and do not get burnt.

The vegetables have to be stir-fried, until they are almost cooked and yet retain their crunchiness and crispiness. Stir-frying vegetables on high heat takes about 4 to 6 minutes.

Add the soy sauce, salt and pepper. Stir quickly and add cooked and cooled rice. Stir fry for a few minutes until the sauce has coated the rice well. Keep a check when adding salt, as soy sauce already has salt in it.

Serve the fried rice hot as it is or with your favorite Chinese side.

Serving suggestions

Though fried rice tastes great on its own, you can pair it with Veg Manchurian, Gobi Manchurian, Chilli Paneer, Spring Rolls or Chilli Mushroom. More side recipes for veg fried rice are linked and listed in the main post.

Storing fried rice

Vegetable fried rice stays good for a couple of days. But I would recommend it to be eaten as soon as you can since many days old rice is not good for health.

Notes

Ingredient Notes

Rice: Aged, long-grained, non-sticky white rice is the best to make fried rice. Here I have used basmati rice.

Veggies: You can add your favorite vegetables or mushrooms in a total quantity of 1.5 to 2 cups finely chopped mixed vegetables excluding mushrooms. You can vary the amount of each veggie as you like.

Protein: Include tofu, seitan, tempeh, or for a vegetarian option, add paneer.

Mushrooms: Swap button mushrooms for cremini or shiitake mushrooms. Skip if you do not have them.

Celery: Omit adding celery, if you do not have it.

Soy sauce: Preferably use naturally brewed soy sauce. For gluten-free fried rice, use tamari or Braggs liquid aminos.

Oils: Peanut, sunflower, avocado oil are good options as they have a high smoking point which suits stir-frying at high heat.

Recipe Notes

Cooking rice: Do not overcook the rice. You only want the rice to be al dente. Always drain and completely cool rice before adding it to the stir-fried vegetables. Wet or hot rice will end up being soggy.

Flavors and seasonings: Add a bit of tomato ketchup for a slightly sweet flavor. To make spicy fried rice, add some red chili sauce or green chili sauce along with the soy sauce.

Soggy and mushy rice: Drain your rice thoroughly. There shouldn't be any water in them. Cooked rice has to be cooled completely before you begin stir-frying. Soft or overdone rice breaks when stir-frying and becomes mushy.

Reheating fried rice: I usually steam them in my Instant-pot for 5 minutes. Sometimes I also stir-fry them in a skillet sprinkling a few splashes of water, so that the rice grains do not dry out.: Swap button mushrooms for cremini or shiitake mushrooms. Skip if you do not have them.

Celery: Omit adding celery, if you do not have it.

Soy sauce: Preferably use naturally brewed soy sauce. For gluten-free fried rice, use tamari or Braggs liquid aminos.

Oils: Peanut, sunflower, avocado oil are good options as they have a high smoking point which suits stir-frying at high heat.

Tomato Rice (Thakkali Sadam)

This quick, delicious Tomato Rice recipe is a favorite dish from the Tamil Nadu state of South India. Also known as Thakkali Sadam, this one pot wonder is tasty, healthy and perfect to pack in a tiffin for lunch on the go.

Prep Time   :   20 mins

Cook Time   :   20 mins

Total Time   :   40 mins

Cuisine   :   South Indian

Servings   :   3

Ingredients

For soaking rice

1 heaped cup basmati rice or any regular rice

water as required

<u>More ingredients</u>

1 cup finely chopped tomatoes (tightly packed) or 3 medium to large tomatoes or 200 grams

⅓ cup finely chopped onions or 1 medium-sized onion

1.5 teaspoons Ginger-Garlic Paste or 1 inch ginger + 5 to 6 small to medium garlic crushed in mortar-pestle

½ teaspoon chopped green chilli or serrano pepper or 1 green chilli

½ teaspoon mustard seeds

4 to 5 fenugreek seeds (methi seeds) - optional

½ inch true cinnamon

2 green cardamoms

2 to 3 cloves

6 to 7 curry leaves (medium-sized)

¼ teaspoon turmeric powder

½ teaspoon red chilli powder

½ teaspoon black pepper powder or crushed black pepper

½ teaspoon coriander powder (ground coriander)

1 teaspoon cumin powder (ground cumin)

½ tablespoon chopped mint leaves

¼ cup chopped coriander leaves (cilantro)

1.5 to 1.75 cups water or add as required

2 tablespoons oil - any neutral oil

salt as required

Instructions

__Preparation__

Rinse basmati rice or any regular rice for a couple of times in water.

Then soak the rice in water for 20 to 30 minutes. Later drain the rice and keep aside.

Chop the tomatoes, onions and green chillies finely. Peel and crush the ginger-garlic in a mortar pestle. Also, chop the mint and coriander leaves

Keep aside all the spices required for the rice.

Sautéing onions, tomatoes, spices

In a 3 litre pressure cooker, heat the oil. Keep the flame to a low and add mustard seeds and crackle them. Then add fenugreek seeds and just lightly fry for a couple of seconds without burning them.

Then add finely chopped onions and cinnamon, cardamoms and cloves.

Stir and sauté until the onions turn translucent and soften.

Add the ginger-garlic paste, chopped green chilies and curry leaves.

Stir and sauté for some seconds until the raw aroma of ginger-garlic goes away

Now add chopped mint leaves and coriander leaves.

Stir and saute for a minute.

Keep heat to a low or switch off the heat. Add the finely chopped tomatoes and turmeric powder, red chilli powder, black pepper powder or crushed black pepper, coriander powder and cumin powder.

Mix very well and sauté the tomatoes until they soften and become pulpy with oil releasing from the sides.

__Cooking tomato rice__

Add the soaked rice. Gently mix the rice with the tomato mixture very well.

Sauté for a minute.

Add 1.75 cups of water. For a more softer consistency in the rice, you can also add 2 cups of water.

Season with salt as per taste.

Cover and pressure cook tomato rice for 2 whistles on medium flame or about 10 to 11 minutes. To get a softer rice, you can also pressure cook for 3 whistles.

When the pressure settles down on its own. Then remove the lid and gently fluff the tomato rice.

Serve tomato rice with appalams or chips or with a side raita.

<u>Notes</u>

<u>Recipe Tips</u>

<u>Reducing spiciness:</u> To reduce the heat and pungency, use less amounts of ginger-garlic paste, black pepper powder and red chili powder. So you can add 1 teaspoon ginger-garlic paste, ¼ teaspoon red chilli powder and ¼ teaspoon black pepper powder.

<u>Quantity of water:</u> I have added 1¾ cup water as this amount was perfect for the basmati rice that I had used. The amount of water that you need to add will also depend on the quality of rice. For a softer rice you can add 2 cups and for separate grains, add 1½ cup water.

<u>Scaling</u>: While you can make this recipe for a larger group, increasing the ingredients proportionally may not work for this recipe.

<u>Cooking in a pan:</u> Start out with 2 cups of water to cook the rice, then cover with a lid and simmer. Check when the rice is about halfway done, and if it looks dry, add up to another ¼ cup of water.

<u>Cooking in an Instant Pot</u>: Begin with setting the sauté function for the steps of sautéing spices, onion and tomatoes. After you add the rice and water, put the lid on and switch the function to pressure cook on high for 6 to 8 minutes, then allow a natural release after 10 minutes.

<u>**Ingredient Swaps**</u>

<u>**Cooked rice**</u>: You can skip adding raw rice. If you have leftover rice or cooked rice, then mix it with the tomato masala and mix thoroughly. You can add about 3 ½ to 4 cups of cooked rice.

<u>**Canned tomatoes:**</u> You could easily add 1 cup of chopped or crushed canned tomatoes in place of fresh tomatoes.

Lemon Rice | Chitranna Recipe

Lemon Rice also known as chitranna or nimmakaya pulihora is a crunchy, flavorful and tangy rice dish that is easy to make and tastes so good.

Prep Time   : 20 mins

Cook Time   : 5 mins

Total Time   : 25 mins

Cuisine   : South Indian

Servings   : 3

Ingredients

<u>**For cooking rice**</u>

1 cup rice (heaped) or 3 to 4 cups cooked rice

1.75 to 2 cups water

¼ teaspoon salt or add as required

<u>**Other ingredients**</u>

1.5 to 2 tablespoons lemon juice or add as required

1 teaspoon mustard seeds

1 teaspoon urad dal (spilt and skinned black gram)

2 dry red chilies - preferably seeds removed

1 teaspoon chopped green chilies or 1 to 2 green chillies - chopped

12 to 15 curry leaves

1 generous pinch asafoetida (hing)

½ teaspoon turmeric powder

1 tablespoon cashews - halved or chopped (optional)

¼ cup peanuts - optional

3 tablespoons sesame oil (gingelly oil) or any neutral oil

salt as required

Instructions

Soaking rice

Rinse rice grains a couple of times and soak in enough water for 20 to 30 minutes.

Then drain all the water from the soaked rice.

Stove-top pressure cooking

Cook rice in a 2-litre or 3-litre pressure cooker with salt and 1.75 to 2 cups water for 2 to 3 whistles or 8 to 10 minutes on medium to medium-high heat.

When the pressure settles down on its own in the cooker, remove the lid. Remove the cooked rice in a plate or in a bowl.

1 heaped cup rice will yield 3 to 4 cups of rice. This will depend on the type and quality of rice.

Let the cooked rice become warm or cool at room temperature

Cooking rice a pan or pot

Take rice, salt and 2 cups of water in a pan. Cover and simmer until all the water has been absorbed and rice grains are tender and fluffy.

Do keep a check when rice is simmering and if the water has dried leaving the rice grains undercooked, add some more hot water and continue to cook.

Place the cooked rice in a tray or bowl to cool it.

Instant pot method

Add rice, salt and 1 or 1.25 cups water (depending on rice type and quality) in the steel insert of a 6 quart IP.

Pressure cook for 5 minutes on high. Do a quick pressure release after 5 minutes.

Empty the cooked rice in a plate or bowl to cool at room temperature.

Frying nuts

In a small frying pan, heat 2 tablespoons of sesame oil. First fry the peanuts until crunchy and then set them aside.

In the same oil, then fry cashews until golden. Remove and set aside.

Now add 1 tablespoon sesame oil in the same pan. Keep the flame to a low.

Add the mustard seeds and let them crackle. Once the mustard seeds begin to crackle, add the urad dal.

Fry until the urad dal turns golden. Fry everything on a low flame, so that the lentils do not burn.

Then add the red chilies, green chilies (chopped) and curry leaves. Sauté for a few seconds until the red chilies change color.

Switch off the heat and add the asafoetida and turmeric powder. Mix very well

Making lemon rice

Immediately pour this tempering mixture on cooked and cooled rice. Add the fried peanuts and cashews, lemon juice, salt. Mix very well.

Keep the bowl or pan covered for the flavors to blend for 4 to 5 minutes.

Then serve the lemon rice.

While serving you can choose to garnish chitranna with some chopped coriander leaves (cilantro).

Serving suggestions

Serve lemon rice with poppadoms or with a side vegetable salad or even coconut chutney also goes great with this dish.

It can also be packed in the tiffin box. As lemon rice can be served at room temperature, it also makes a great picnic lunch item. It's a light dish and you can have it as a light lunch or breakfast too.

Storing

Leftovers can be stored in the refrigerator for a day. Leftover rice is not good for health, so I suggest to finish the lemon rice in a day.

Notes

Rice: Any non-sticky variety of rice can be added. If in case you overcook the rice and they become lumpy, then do not worry. Simply break the lumps when the rice grains are cooled. Leftover rice works excellently in the recipe. Add about 3 to 4 cups of leftover cooked rice.

Spices and lentils: Spices like mustard seeds and either dry red chillies or green chillies are essential. You can still let go of urad dal and asafoetida (hing) if they are not available to you. About 1 teaspoon of finely chopped ginger also adds a good flavor to the chitranna recipe.

Herbs: Curry leaves add a unique aroma. If you find it difficult to procure them, then you can skip them. You can also add coriander leaves (cilantro).

Nuts: Both cashews and peanuts add a lot of texture and crunch in lemon rice. You can also just use one type of nut. Do not use nuts like almonds, pistachios, pecans, walnuts etc as the authenticity of the recipe will be lost.

Lemons: Use lemons or limes which are ripe and fresh.

Oil: The oil that is traditionally used in sesame oil made from wood pressed raw sesame seeds. This sesame oil, also known as gingelly oil is very different from the south-asian toasted sesame oil. If you do not have sesame oil, then simply use sunflower oil, peanut oil, avocado oil, grapeseed oil or any neutral oil.

Gluten-free version: To make a gluten-free lemon rice simply skip the asafetida or use a gluten-free asafetida.

Peas Pulao | Matar Pulao

Peas pulao also known as matar pulao is a tasty rice and green peas dish made with caramelized onions and aromatic spices. It can be prepared entirely in a stove-top pressure cooker or in a pan or in the Instant pot. I share all three ways to make this delish peas pulao.

Prep Time   :   10 mins

Cook Time   :   15 mins

Total Time   :   25 mins

Cuisine   :   Indian, Punjabi

Servings   :   3

Ingredients

Main ingredients

1 cup basmati rice (heaped), 200 grams

¾ cup green peas (matar) - preferably fresh or frozen

½ cup thinly sliced onions

3 tablespoons oil or ghee (clarified butter)

1.75 cups water for stove-top pressure cooking

salt as required

Whole spices

1 teaspoon cumin seeds

1 inch cinnamon

1 black cardamom - optional

1 or 2 green cardamom

2 to 3 cloves

1 or 2 mace strands - thin strands, optional

1 medium-sized tej patta (Indian bay leaf)

Instructions

Preparation

Wash the basmati rice until the water runs clear of the starch.

Soak rice for 30 minutes.

Drain all the water and set aside.

Making peas pulao

Heat oil or ghee in a 2-litre pressure cooker.

Add the cumin seeds along with all the whole spices. Fry for some seconds on low heat, until the spices splutter, release their aroma and become fragrant, taking care not to burn them

Then add the sliced onions. Stir and sauté until the onions are light golden or caramelized. Do not burn the onions as this will lead to a bitter taste in your matar pulao.

Add the green peas and saute for a minute.

Then add the drained rice and mix gently.

Sauté for a minute seeing that the fat (oil or ghee) coats the rice grains. Add water and salt as required. Mix well. Check the taste of water and it should be slightly salty.

Cover and pressure cook for 2 whistles or 6 to 7 minutes on a medium-high to high heat. Let the pressure settle down on its own and then open the lid of the cooker. If you like your rice more on the al dente side then only pressure cook for 1 whistle.

Gently fluff rice and serve peas pulao hot or warm.

Serving suggestions

Enjoy peas pulao on their own as a side or main dish, or serve with nearly any condiments or sides. The peas and rice pair perfectly with creamy and cool yogurt sauces and dips, like onion tomato raita, cucumber raita or boondi raita.

Matar pulao also goes well with fresh Curd (Yogurt) as such and a Kadhi Pakora, sliced onion rings, Indian onion-tomato salad (Kachumber), and/or mango or lemon pickle. You can even serve with a side of lemon wedges.

For an even heartier meal, peas pulao can be served with fried or roasted or masala papad, a simple Gujarati Kadhi, or Pakora.

Notes

Cooking peas pulao in a pan

Follow the recipe directions, until you add water and salt. You will have to add 2 to 2.25 cups of water. Cover the pan or pot tightly with a lid and simmer until all of the water is absorbed and the rice grains are cooked through.

Do keep a check on the rice when they are cooking. If the water has been all absorbed and rice grains have not yet cooked completely, add a few tablespoons of water. Cover and cook rice for a few minutes.

Instant Pot Method

In the steel insert pot of a 6 quart IP, fry the whole spices and sauté onions until they caramelize. Add the green peas, rice, 1.5 cups of water, and salt.

Pressure cook on high for 5 minutes. Wait for 10 minutes after the pressure cooking is completed and the beep sound is heard. Release any extra pressure after 10 minutes.

Keep a note of the 10 minutes time and do not allow it to exceed it. The rice grains may get overdone and become mushy.

Ingredient Notes

Type of rice: Aged basmati rice will give your pulao the best taste and texture. If you do not have basmati rice, include any non-sticky variety of long-grained or medium-grained rice.

Whole spices: Try to add all the whole spices mentioned in the recipe. If not readily available you can feel free to leave out the black cardamom and mace. The dish won't have quite the same smoky and earthy flavor but will still be quite delicious.

Herbs: Including herbs like coriander leaves (cilantro) or mint or equal combinations of both, also gives a good herby taste and flavor. Add about 3 tablespoons of either or 2 tablespoons each of both chopped coriander and mint leaves. For dried mint, add about 1 teaspoon of it.

Cooking Notes

Rice to water proportion: While cooking in a pressure cooker, 1½ to 1¾ cups of water works perfectly for every 1 cup of basmati rice. But depending on the quality of rice you can add less or more water - from 1½ cups to 2 cups.

Spiciness: This recipe is not spicy. To make a spicy matar pulao, you can add some green chilies and 1 teaspoon ginger-garlic paste.

Color: The color of matar pulao here is slightly brown due to the caramelization created when frying the onions. I strongly recommend caramelizing the onions as it gives lovely sweet undertones to the dish. But, if you'd like a white-colored pulao, then instead of caramelizing you can sauté the onions until translucent. You can also add a few drops of lemon juice which will help maintain the rice's white color.

Paneer Biryani Recipe

Paneer biryani is a mildly spiced and delicately flavored dum cooked, traditional biryani recipe. It pairs beautifully with any raita or even with simple plain curd (yogurt).

Prep Time   :   45 mins

Cook Time   :   20 mins

Total Time   :   1 hr 5 mins

Cuisine   :   Awadhi, North Indian

Servings   :   3

Ingredients

For barista or fried onions

1 cup thinly sliced onions - 150 grams or 2 medium to large-sized onions

4 tablespoon oil or ghee (clarified butter)

For cooking rice

1 cup basmati rice - 180 grams, preferably aged basmati rice

4 cups water

1 teaspoon salt

1 inch cinnamon (dalchini)

1 tej patta (medium-sized) or 2 small tej patta

2 to 3 cloves

2 to 3 green cardamoms

¼ teaspoon shahjeera (caraway seeds)

<u>**For paneer marination**</u>

200 to 250 grams Paneer (cottage cheese)

½ cup Curd (yogurt)

1 teaspoon ginger paste or 1 inch ginger crushed to a paste in a mortar-pestle

1 teaspoon garlic paste or 4 to 5 garlic medium-sized cloves crushed to a paste

1 teaspoon chopped green chilies or serrano pepper or 1 to 2 green chillies

1 tablespoon chopped coriander leaves (cilantro)

½ tablespoon chopped mint leaves

¼ teaspoon turmeric powder (ground turmeric)

¼ teaspoon red chili powder or cayenne pepper

¼ teaspoon Garam Masala Powder

½ teaspoon coriander powder

(ground coriander)

¼ teaspoon shahjeera (caraway seeds)

1 teaspoon lemon juice

salt as required

<u>**Layering ingredients**</u>

¼ cup milk

16 to 18 saffron strands

1 to 2 tablespoons ghee (clarified butter)

1 tablespoon chopped coriander leaves (cilantro)

½ tablespoon chopped mint leaves

1 tablespoon rose water or kewra water (pandanus water) - optional

Instructions

Cooking rice

Rinse basmati rice very well in water till the starch clears from the water. The water should be clear and not cloudy or opaque.

Then soak the rice in water for 30 minutes. Later drain the rice well and keep aside.

Bring 4 cups of water to a rolling boil in a pot.

Add whole spices - cinnamon, tej patta, cloves , green cardamoms, caraway seeds. Also add salt.

Now add the soaked rice. Do not stir the rice.

Keep the flame high and cook the rice without lowering the temperature.

The rice grains have to be cooked till 75% or ¾ done. They should have a bite to them when eaten.

Drain the rice in a colander. You can also rinse the rice grains to remove starch if any and to stop the grains from cooking. Cover with a lid and keep the rice aside.

Making barista or fried onions

When the rice is soaking, prep the ingredients for the biryani. Slice the onions. Heat the oil or ghee in a small frying pan and add the sliced onions.

Stir and begin to fry the onions till they turn golden. Add one or two pinches of salt for quick browning of the onions. Stir often for uniform browning and fry on a low flame.

Here the onions have begun to get golden.

Once the onions become golden, then remove them with a slotted spoon and place them on kitchen paper towels. Keep the fried onions aside.

Preparation for marination

Warm the milk on stove top or in the microwave. Add 16 to 18 saffron strands to the milk. Stir and keep aside.

Whisk full fat curd (yogurt) in a mixing bowl till smooth.

Add ginger paste, garlic paste, chopped green chilies, chopped coriander leaves and mint leaves. Mix well.

Now add the spices- turmeric powder, red chili powder, garam masala powder, coriander powder, caraway seeds and lemon juice.

And salt as required. Mix again.

Then add the half of the fried onions and the paneer cubes.

Mix gently. Cover and keep the marinated paneer aside for 30 minutes.

Assembling and layering

Add the same oil in which we fried the onions to a pan or pot.

Add the marinated paneer and layer neatly.

Make a rice layer now. Add all the rice. I have just made two layers. If you want you can make four layers.

Add the remaining fried onions, chopped coriander and mint leaves.

Sprinkle the saffron infused milk.

Dot with ghee. You can also add rose water or kewra water.

Dum cooking paneer biryani

Cover with aluminium foil or with a moist kitchen cotton towel or napkin.

Place the lid tightly on the pan and place it on a tava or griddle. For the first 5 minutes dum cook the paneer biryani on a medium flame.

Then lower the flame and cook the paneer biryani

On dum for 12 to 15 minutes. You can also cook the paneer biryani in a preheated oven for 20 to 25 minutes at 180 degrees Celsius. Use an oven proof pan.

Serve the paneer biryani hot with boondi raita or cucumber raita or onion tomato raita or kachumber salad.

Serving Suggestions

Enjoy paneer biryani hot or warm with raita like an onion-tomato raita or cucumber raita or boondi raita. You can also serve with sliced onion-lime salad or onion-tomato-cucumber salad.

Pairing it with curries like mirchi ka salan and bagara baingan also tastes awesome. Even a simple plain yogurt tastes nice with it.

Storage

Place any leftovers in any sealed box or container and refrigerate for 1 to 2 days. Reheat by warming in the oven at 90 degrees Celsius (195 degrees Fahrenheit) or by steaming in the Instant pot for 5 minutes.

Notes

Ingredient Variations

Rice: For biryani I usually prefer aged basmati rice as the grains become fluffy, tender and non-sticky when cooked. Parboiled basmati rice (sella basmati rice) is yet another rice variety I like to make biryani with. You can make paneer biryani with any long grained variety of non-sticky rice.

Adding veggies: You can add some steamed peas and steamed veggies like carrots, cauliflower, potatoes. But then you will have to increase the curd and other spices accordingly to accommodate the veggies.

Vegan option: For a vegan version of paneer biryani, use tofu, oil and a dairy free yogurt & milk like cashew or almond milk/yogurt. Avoid soy or peanut yogurt as it gives an aftertaste.

Nuts and dried fruits: Fried cashews and raisins can also be added in the layers.

Whole spices: I recommend adding all the spices and herbs in the same proportion as listed in the recipe. The only suggestion I offer which will alter the flavor slightly will be to replace caraway seeds (shah jeera) with cumin seeds.

<u>**Cooking Notes**</u>

<u>**Cooking rice:**</u> Do not cook the rice grains completely. They have to be slightly underdone. Fully cooked rice grains will end up with a mushy biryani as the rice grains cook further during the dum cooking process.

<u>**Paneer**</u>: Use homemade paneer for best taste and texture. For frozen paneer, thaw them in warm or hot water for a few minutes.

<u>**Marinating time**</u>: I always marinate the paneer for 30 minutes at room temperature. The paneer cubes can also be marinated for a few hours or overnight in the refrigerator.

<u>**Making barista**</u>: The barista or fried onions can be made a day before and stored in an airtight container. You can also make a big batch of fried onions which come in handy when making biryani. Freeze them for a longer storage.

Mushroom Biryani

This is a spicy, tasty one-pot mushroom biryani recipe from the Chettinad cuisine. You can make this mushroom biryani on the stove-top in a pan or pressure cooker and in the Instant Pot as well with my instructions listed in the recipe card.

Prep Time   : 30 mins

Cook Time   : 25 mins

Total Time   : 55 mins

Cuisine   : Chettinad, South Indian

Servings   : 3

Ingredients

<u>**For marinating rice**</u>

1 cup basmati rice (heaped) - 200 grams or seeraga samba rice

1 teaspoon ghee for marinating rice

For ground green masala paste

¼ cup chopped mint leaves

¼ cup chopped coriander leaves (cilantro)

3 to 4 green chilies

3 to 4 garlic cloves - small to medium-sized

½ inch ginger

½ tablespoon water

For marinating mushrooms

200 to 250 grams white button mushrooms - quartered

3 tablespoons Curd (yogurt)

¼ to ⅓ teaspoon turmeric powder (ground turmeric)

½ teaspoon red chilli powder or cayenne pepper

½ teaspoon Garam Masala Powder

1 teaspoon coriander powder (ground coriander)

Other ingredients

2 to 2.5 tablespoons oil - any neutral tasting oil or coconut oil

1 inch cinnamon

2 green cardamoms

3 to 4 cloves

6 to 7 black pepper

1 tejpatta - medium to large-sized (Indian bay leaf)

2 single strands of mace

1 stone flower - small piece, (dagad phool aur patthar phool) - optional

2 marathi moggu (kapok buds) - optional

1 teaspoon fennel seeds

2 onions (medium-sized) - 100 grams, thinly sliced

1 tomato (medium to large) - 80 grams, chopped

½ to 1 cup water or add as required

1 cup thick coconut milk

salt as required

For garnish

2 to 3 tablespoons chopped coriander leaves or 1 to 2 tablespoons mint leaves

Instructions

Prepping rice

First rinse rice very well in water. Then soak the rice in water for 30 minutes.

After 30 minutes, drain the rice and add 1 tsp ghee to it.

Coat the rice with ghee very well and allow to marinate for 20 to 25 minutes. Instead of marinating, you can also saute the rice in ghee lightly.

Preparing veggies and mushrooms

When you keep the rice for soaking, prep the ingredients. First rinse or wipe dry and then quarter the mushrooms. Take the mushroom in a mixing bowl.

Slice thinly 2 medium onions. Chop 1 medium to large tomato. Also chop 3 to 4 green chilies, 3 to 4 medium garlic cloves and ½ inch ginger. Also chop mint and coriander leaves.

Making the ground green paste

In a small grinder or chutney grinder, take the chopped mint leaves, coriander leaves and the chopped green chilies, garlic & ginger.

Add ½ tbsp water and grind to a smooth paste.

Marinating mushrooms

Add the ground paste along with 3 tbsp curd to the chopped mushrooms.

Add turmeric powder, red chilli powder, garam masala powder and coriander powder.

Gently mix all the ingredients with the mushrooms. Cover and keep aside to marinate for 30 to 40 minutes.

Take all the whole spices and keep aside.

Sautéing spices, onions, tomatoes

Heat 2 to 2.5 tbsp oil in a thick bottomed pot or pan. Add the whole spices and fry or sauté them till they are fragrant.

Then add the sliced onions. Stir very well and saute them on a low to medium flame. Add a pinch of salt for quick cooking of the onions.

Stir often and saute till the onions become golden.

Then add tomatoes. Stir and saute the tomatoes for about 2 minutes.

Cooking mushrooms

Add the marinated mushrooms. Stir very well and saute the mushrooms for 6 to 7 minutes or till they shrink and you see oil specks on top.

In the bowl there will be some marinade left. Add 1 cup water and mix the marinade with the water.

Add water as required depending on the quality of rice. You can add from ½ to 1 cup water. Since I used organic basmati rice, I have added 1 cup of water.

Add this water to the mushrooms. then add 1 cup thick coconut milk. Mix well.

Season with salt and stir. On a medium heat bring the mixture to a boil.

Cooking mushroom biryani

Then add the ghee coated rice. Stir well.

Cover the pot or pan with a lid. Check once or twice when rice is cooking.

On sim or low flame cook the biryani till the rice grains are done.

It took me 12 minutes for the rice to cook. Depending on the thickness and depth of the pan, quality of rice and flame intensity, it can take about 10 to 12 minutes to cook the rice.

Once the rice grains are tender, cover and allow to stand for 5 minutes before serving mushroom biryani. Then gently fluff the rice with a fork.

Garnish with mint or coriander leaves and serve mushroom biryani with a side salad or raita.

Notes

Ingredient Notes

Rice: This biryani tastes good with both basmati rice and seeraga samba rice. If you do not have either of these rice varieties, then make mushroom biryani with any non-sticky variety of short-grained or medium-sized rice.

Spices: For the best flavor and taste, I would suggest to use all spices. But due to non availability, skip kapok buds, stone flower and mace.

Vegan options: Use vegan yogurt in place of dairy yogurt or skip the curd (yogurt) altogether. If skipping yogurt, then add 1 teaspoon lemon juice to the rice after adding water. Use a neutral oil in place of ghee.

Mushrooms: Cremini mushrooms and shiitake mushrooms also taste great in this recipe. You can include a combination of various varieties of edible fresh mushrooms.

Cooking notes

Water quantity: Depending on the quality, age of rice and the water content in coconut milk, the amount of water will vary. Usually for 1 cup of basmati rice, 2 cups of liquids work well when cooking in a pan or pot.

Rinsing rice: Do rinse the rice grains well so that the water is clear of starch. This will help in making the cooked rice grains non-sticky.

<u>**Alternative Cooking methods**</u>

You can easily make this dish in a stove-top pressure cooker or in the Instant Pot. Vary the quantity of water and time as required with the kind of rice you are using.

<u>**Instant Pot Method**</u>: For Instant pot, follow the sautéing instructions in the steel insert of your IP using the sauté function. Add 1 cup of coconut milk and ½ cup of water. Season with salt. Combine well. Seal tightly with the IP lid and position the valve to sealing position. Pressure cook on high pressure for 5 minutes. When you hear the beep sound after the pressure cooking is complete, wait for 10 minutes and then do a quick pressure release.

Cooking in Stove-top Pressure Cooker: Follow the sautéing instructions in a 2 litre pressure cooker. Add 1 cup coconut milk, ¾ cup water and season with salt. Pressure cook on medium to medium-high heat for 2 to 3 whistles or 8 to 9 minutes. When the pressure falls naturally in the cooker, open the lid. Fluff and serve.

Corn pulao

Spiced and tasty pulao made with sweet corn.

Prep Time   :   20 mins

Cook Time   :   15 mins

Total Time   :   35 mins

Cuisine   :   Indian

Servings   :   2 to 3

<u>*Ingredients*</u>

<u>main ingredients</u>

1 cup heaped regular rice or basmati rice or 210 to 215 grams rice

1.5 cups corn kernels

2 tablespoon oil

1 medium to large onion, thinly sliced or ½ cup sliced onion

¼ teaspoon turmeric powder

¼ teaspoon red chilli powder

½ teaspoon coriander powder

2 cups water or add as required

salt as required

2 tablespoon chopped coriander leaves for garnish

for the green chutney paste

¼ cup chopped coriander leaves

1 tablespoon chopped mint leaves

½ inch ginger - chopped or ½ teaspoon chopped ginger

1 or 2 green chilies - chopped

3 to 4 small garlic - chopped

1 tablespoon desiccated coconut or fresh coconut

1 to 2 tablespoon water for grinding

whole spices

1 small to medium tej patta (indian bay leaf)

2 green cardamoms

2 to 3 cloves

1 inch cinnamon

1 small star anise (chakri phool) - optional

1 or 2 single strands of mace (javitri)

½ teaspoon cumin seeds

4 to 5 black peppers

1 tiny piece of stone flower (patthar ke phool) - optional

Instructions

preparation

Rinse 1 heaped cup rice well in water and then soak in enough water for 20 minutes.

After 20 minutes strain the rice well and keep aside. I used ambemohar rice (mango blossom rice). You can also use basmati rice or regular rice.

When the rice is soaking, slice the corn kernels from the corn. Keep them aside. From 1 medium corn cob, I got 1.5 cups corn kernels. You can also use 1 cup corn kernels.

making green chutney paste for pulao

Take the ingredients mentioned "for green chutney" in a small grinder or chutney grinder.

Add 1 to 2 tbsp water and grind to a smooth paste. You can skip coconut, if you don't have one. In this case, add 1 to 2 tsp water while grinding.

If not grinding then just add chopped coriander and mint leaves after the onions are browned, directly in the cooker. Also add 1 tsp ginger garlic paste and skip desiccated coconut.

making corn pulao

Heat 2 tbsp oil in a pan. Add all the spices mentioned under the list "whole spices". Allow them to crackle.

Then add the thinly sliced onions. Saute the onion until it starts becoming golden.

Then add the ground paste. Stir well and saute for a couple of seconds.

Then add the corn kernels.

Season with the following spices - 1/4 tsp turmeric powder, 1/4 tsp red chilli powder and 1/2 tsp coriander powder.

Stir very well and add the rice. Gently stir and mix the rice with the rest of the ingredients.

Now add 1.75 to 2 cups of water. Depending on the type and quality of rice, you can add water. For basmati rice, you can add 1.5 to 1.75 cups of water.

Organic basmati rice requires more water to cook. So add 2 cups of water for organic basmati rice. Stir.

Season with salt. Taste and the water should have a slightly salty taste.

Cover and pressure cook corn rice on a medium flame for 2 whistles or for 9 to 12 minutes. Here I pressure cooked for 15 minutes, since ambemohar rice takes a longer time to cook than basmati rice.

When the pressure settles down on its own, remove the lid. Gently fluff the rice.

Garnish with 2 tbsp chopped coriander leaves.

And then serve corn pulao with a side veggie salad or raita.

Schezwan Fried Rice

Schezwan fried rice is a spicy and tasty indo Chinese recipe of stir fried vegetables and rice in schezwan sauce

Prep Time   :   20 mins

Cook Time   : 20 mins

Total Time   : 40 mins

Cuisine   : Indo Chinese

Servings   :   3

Ingredients

For cooking rice

1 cup basmati rice or long grained rice, 200 grams

3.5 cups water

½ teaspoon salt

¼ teaspoon oil - any neutral tasting oil

Other ingredients

2 tablespoons toasted sesame oil or any neutral tasting oil

½ teaspoon finely chopped garlic or 2 to 3 small to medium garlic

1 or 2 spring onions (scallions) - finely chopped, reserve the greens for garnishing

1 teaspoon finely chopped celery (optional)

7 to 8 french beans - finely chopped

⅓ to ½ cup finely chopped carrots or 1 medium-sized carrot

½ cup chopped cabbage

⅓ cup chopped capsicum (green bell pepper) or 1 small capsicum

1 cups chopped button mushrooms - optional

2 tablespoons Schezwan Sauce or add as required

salt as required

¼ teaspoon crushed black pepper or add as required

½ teaspoon rice vinegar or apple cider vinegar or white vinegar

Instructions

Cooking rice

Rinse rice very well till the water runs clear of starch. Soak the rice in enough water for 30 minutes.

Drain and keep aside.

In a pot, bring water to a gentle boil adding salt and oil.

Add the soaked and drained rice to the hot water.

On a low to medium flame cook the rice without the lid.

When the rice becomes al dente or just cooked, remove the pot from fire and strain the rice.

Gently rinse the rice in water so that they stop cooking and don't stick to each other.

Cover the rice and keep aside. You can even cover and refrigerate the rice.

Making schezwan fried rice

Finely chop all the vegetables. You can even shred the vegetables in a food processor.

Heat oil in a wok. Add garlic and saute for 15 to 20 seconds.

Add the onions, celery and all the vegetables.

Increase the flame and stir fry the vegetables on a high heat.

More finely chopped the vegetables are, the faster they will cook.

Keep on stirring and tossing the vegetables on a high heat continuously. So that they are equally browned and cooked.

When the edges of the veggies start to become light brown, add schezwan sauce.

Stir and then add the drained rice in parts. Mix and toss the rice with the veggies gently.

Season with salt, pepper and vinegar. Stir and toss well so that the sauce coats all the rice grains evenly.

Garnish with the spring onions greens.

Serve schezwan fried rice as it is or with a side of veg manchurian, mushroom manchurian or gobi manchurian.

Notes

Smoky Flavor: Stir frying at a very high heat and continuously stirring the ingredients in the wok aids in giving a smoky flavor to the dish.

Prepping: Be sure to have all your sauces and seasonings prepared before you begin the stir-frying.

Al dente rice: Another key point is to steam or cook the rice and let it cool completely. The rice has to be cooked al dente, meaning just about cooked.

Veggies: The veggies can be shredded, julienned or chopped finely.

Schezwan Sauce: Make your own homemade schezwan sauce or use a good brand. The amount of schezwan sauce to be added depends on the spice level in the sauce and your taste buds so add less or more according to your taste buds.

Veg tehri recipe

Veg tahiri recipe - spiced one pot rice dish made with vegetables and spices. A specialty from Uttar Pradesh cuisine.

Prep Time   : 20 mins

Cook Time   : 30 mins

Total Time   : 50 mins

Cuisine   : Awadhi, North Indian, Uttar Pradesh

Servings   : 4 to 5

Ingredients

veggies for veg tehri

200 to 210 grams potatoes, 2 large potatoes or 1 cup tightly packed potatoes

200 to 210 grams cauliflower, 2 cups chopped cauliflower florets

115 grams carrots or 2 medium sized or ½ cup chopped carrots

50 grams french beans or 12 to 14 french beans or 1/3 cup chopped beans

½ cup green peas - fresh or frozen

other ingredients for veg tehri

3 tablespoon ghee

175 grams onions or 3 medium sized onions or 1 cup heaped sliced onions

155 grams tomatoes or 3 medium sized tomatoes or ¾ cup chopped tomatoes

1 tablespoon Ginger-Garlic Paste or 1 inch ginger + 6 to 7 garlic - crushed to a paste in mortar-pestle

1 tablespoon chopped mint leaves

3 tablespoon chopped coriander leaves

3 green chilies - slit

1 teaspoon red chilli powder

1 teaspoon coriander powder

½ teaspoon turmeric powder

1.5 cups basmati rice or 300 grams basmati rice

½ tablespoon lemon juice

1 teaspoon kewra water or rose water (optional)

3 cups water

salt as required

whole spices

1 tej patta (indian bay leaf)

4 green cardamoms

2 black cardamoms

4 to 5 cloves

2 sticks each of 1 inch cinnamon

Instructions

preparation for veg tehri recipe

Rinse 1.5 cups basmati rice in water very well till the water runs clear of starch. Then soak the rice in enough water for 30 minutes.

After 30 minutes, drain the rice and keep aside.

Rinse and soak 2 cups mediums sized cauliflower florets in hot water for 15 to 20 minutes.

This blanching step is optional and only to get rid of any insects or worms in the cauliflower. After blanching the cauliflower, drain them and keep aside. Also chop the rest of the veggies and keep aside.

making vegetable tehri

Heat 3 tbsp ghee in a thick bottomed deep pot or pan.

Add the following spices and saute till the spices splutter and become fragrant - 1 tej patta, 4 green cardamoms, 2 black cardamoms, 4 to 5 cloves and 2 sticks each of 1 inch cinnamon. Instead of ghee you can also use mustard oil or sunflower oil.

Then add 1 cup heaped sliced onions.

Stir and begin to saute the onions.

Sauteing the onions takes a lot of time. So add a pinch of salt for quick cooking of the onions.

Saute till the onions become golden.

Then add 1 tbsp ginger+garlic paste. Saute for a few seconds till the raw aroma of ginger and garlic goes away.

Add 3/4 cup chopped tomatoes. Saute the tomatoes for a minute or two.

Then add 1 cup tightly packed diced potatoes. Saute the potatoes for 3 to 4 minutes on a low to medium flame.

Next add 1/2 cup chopped carrots, 1/3 cup chopped french beans , 1/2 cup fresh or frozen green peas and the cauliflower florets.

Mix the veggies with the rest of the ingredients.

Then add 1 tbsp chopped mint leaves, 3 tbsp chopped coriander leaves, 3 slit green chilies, 1 tsp red chilli powder, 1 tsp coriander powder and 1/2 tsp turmeric powder.

Stir and mix very well. add 1/2 tbsp lemon juice.

Then add rice. Mix the rice very well with the masala and saute for a minute.

cooking veg tehri

Pour 3 cups of water. You can also add 1 tsp rose water or kewra water at this step. season with salt.

Cover the pan with a tight lid. If you want you can also seal the pan with an aluminium foil and then cover the pan with a lid.

On a low flame, cook the tahiri till all the water is absorbed and the rice grains are fluffy and soft.

It took me 20 minutes for the rice to cook. Time will vary depending on the size and volume of pan, the thickness of pan, flame intensity etc.

Once done, give a resting time of 5 minutes. Then gently fluff and serve vegetable tahiri with a raita or plain curd.

Palak Biryani

Palak biryani is a lightly spiced, aromatic and easy spinach biryani. A one pot palak biryani that tastes great paired with a veggie salad or raita.

Prep Time   :   30 mins

Cook Time   :   20 mins

Total Time   : 50 mins

Cuisine   :   Indian

Servings   :   4

<u>Ingredients</u>

<u>Main ingredients</u>

2 cups basmati rice - soaked for 30 minutes

1 onion (large) - thinly sliced

1 teaspoon Ginger-Garlic Paste

1 tomato (medium-sized) - chopped

3.5 to 4 cups water or as required

3 tablespoons oil

12 to 15 fried cashews (optional), for garnish

salt as required

<u>Whole spices</u>

1 inch cinnamon

1 star anise (small-sized) - optional

2 green cardamoms

1 or 2 black cardamoms

2 to 3 cloves

1 tej patta (medium-sized)

1 to 2 strands mace

Ground spice powders

¼ teaspoon red chili powder

¼ teaspoon Garam Masala Powder

¼ teaspoon turmeric powder (ground turmeric)

½ teaspoon cumin

1 teaspoon fennel powder (ground fennel)

1 teaspoon coriander powder (ground coriander)

1 pinch asafoetida (hing) - optional

For making palak puree

1 medium bunch of spinach

½ cup mint leaves

½ cup coriander leaves

1 or 2 green chilies

5 to 6 almonds

Instructions

Making palak puree

Rinse the palak (spinach leaves) very well in water.

Chop and keep aside. Rinse & chop the green chilies, mint and coriander leaves

In a blender, add the chopped spinach, mint, coriander, green chili and almonds.

Add ½ cup water and blend to a smooth paste.

Sautéing onions

First rinse and then soak the rice. When the rice is soaking, prepare the spinach puree as mentioned above.

Heat oil in a thick bottom and deep pan or pot. Add all the whole spices.

Fry for some seconds or till the oil gets fragrant.

Add the sliced onions & fry till they are browned. Remove some of the fried onions for garnishing.

Add the ginger-garlic paste and fry for some seconds. Now add hing and saute for a few seconds.

Sautéing tomatoes and spinach puree

Add the chopped tomatoes and sauté till the tomatoes become soft for 2 to 3 minutes.

Keep on stirring so that the ingredients do not stick to the bottom of the pan.

Add the spinach puree and stir. Sauté for 3 to 4 minutes. Now all the dry spice powders one by one and stir.

Add salt as required. Drain the soaked rice and add. Stir for 1 to 2 minutes. Pour 3.5 or 4 cups of water.

Check the taste of the broth and if required add some more salt.

Cooking palak biryani

Cover tightly with a lid and cook till the water is absorbed and the rice is tender and fluffy. Fluff the rice.

Serve palak biryani hot garnished with the fried onions and fried cashews with a side vegetable curry, raita, yogurt curry or some salad.

You can also garnish with herbs like coriander (cilantro) or mint leaves.

Notes

Ingredient Notes & Swaps

Spinach: Both regular spinach and baby spinach can be used to make this palak biryani recipe. You can also use frozen spinach. Thaw and squeeze out the extra water before using your frozen spinach.

Rice: I do suggest to use Basmati rice when making this biryani. But if you do not have basmati rice, then any other variety of long grained rice or even medium-grained rice like sona masuri can be used.

Nuts: Use cashews if you do have almonds for making the spinach puree.

Vegetarian option: To make the biryani vegetarian, use ghee instead of oil. You can use any neutral-flavored oil.

Gluten free option: Skip the asafoetida for a gluten free variation.

Veggies: Add vegetables like french beans, potatoes, green peas, carrots, cauliflower, broccoli to make a healthy variation of this dish. You can also include mushrooms.

Cooking Notes

Water quantity: The amount of water will vary according to the type and age of rice. For 2 cups of basmati rice, 4 cups of water work perfectly when cooking in a pan. In this recipe you can add 3.5 to 4 cups of water (as spinach puree will also have some water in it) depending on the size of pan and rice quality.

Blanching spinach: If you prefer you can blanch the spinach prior to blending. Do not water while blending blanched spinach.

Pressure cooker method: To save time you can cook spinach biryani in a 3-litre pressure cooker. Simply add 3 to 3.25 cups water when using a pressure cooker. Pressure cook on medium to medium-high heat for 9 to 10 minutes or 3 whistles.

Coriander Rice

Coriander rice is an aromatic and spiced rice dish made with fresh cilantro leaves, rice, veggies, herbs and spices.

Prep Time   : 30 mins

Cook Time   : 15 mins

Total Time   : 45 mins

Cuisine   : Indian

Servings   : 2 to 3

Ingredients

main ingredients

1 cup basmati rice, rinsed and soaked in water for 30 minutes

2 tablespoon oil

1 tej patta (indian bay leaf)

2 to 3 cloves

4 to 5 black peppers

½ inch cinnamon

2 green cardamoms

1 or 2 single strands of mace

1 medium onion, thinly sliced or 1/3 cup thinly sliced onions

1 pinch turmeric powder (ground turmeric)

1 medium potato, peeled and chopped

1/3 cup green peas - fresh or frozen

1.5 cups water

salt as required

for the coriander paste

½ cup chopped coriander leaves (cilantro leaves)

2 to 3 green chilies - chopped

½ inch ginger - chopped

2 tablespoon unsweetened desiccated coconut or 2 tablespoon grated coconut

3 to 4 medium garlic - chopped

½ teaspoon cumin seeds

½ teaspoon fennel seeds

2 to 3 tablespoon water for grinding

Instructions

prepping rice

Rinse and then soak rice in water for 30 minutes.

Then drain the water and keep the rice aside. Prep the other ingredients when the rice is soaking.

making coriander paste

Take 1/2 cup chopped coriander leaves (cilantro), 2 to 3 green chilies (chopped), 1/2 inch ginger (chopped), 2 tbsp unsweetened desiccated coconut (or 2 tbsp grated coconut), 3 to 4 medium garlic (chopped), 1/2 tsp cumin seeds (jeera) and 1/2 tsp fennel seeds/saunf in a small grinder or chutney grinder.

Add 2 to 3 tbsp water and grind to a smooth paste. Keep this green paste aside.

Making coriander rice

Heat 2 tbsp oil in a pressure cooker.

Add the following whole spices - 2 to 3 cloves, 4 to 5 black peppers, 1/2 inch cinnamon, 2 green cardamoms and 1 or 2 single strands of mace. Saute till the spices become fragrant. Takes a few seconds.

Add 1/3 cup thinly sliced onions. On a low to medium flame, stir and saute the onions till they become golden.

Keep on stirring often so that the onions have a uniform golden color and do not get burnt.

Lower the flame and add the ground coriander-spices paste. Add a pinch of turmeric powder. Stir very well.

Add chopped 1 medium potato and 1/3 cup green peas. You can use any mixed vegetables of your choice or even skip them. Stir again.

Then add the drained rice. Stir gently and saute the rice for a minute.

Cooking coriander rice

Add 1.5 cups of water and salt. Stir again. Taste the stock and it should feel a bit salty.

Cover and pressure cook rice for 2 whistles or for 9 to 10 minutes on a medium to high flame.

When the pressure settles down on its own, remove the lid and gently fluff the rice.

Serve coriander rice hot with side raita or salad or a pickle. It can also be packed in a tiffin box and will make for a very healthy meal.

Notes

The entire coriander rice recipe can also be made in a pot or pan. Add 2 cups of water if cooking in a pot. Cover tightly and cook the rice grains till done. Do check while the rice is cooking and if required, you can add more water.

If you want then you can skip adding the veggies.

I personally like to add spare veggies to this recipe as it makes the dish more healthy, nutritious and also more flavorful. The veggies that can be added are potatoes, green peas, beans, cauliflower, broccoli, bell pepper, baby corn, brinjal and carrots.

The recipe can be doubled.

Carrot Rice Recipe

Carrot rice is a lightly spiced and delicious rice recipe and can be made quickly. It also goes well as tiffin box lunch.

Prep Time   : 15 mins

Cook Time   : 15 mins

Total Time   : 30 mins

Cuisine   : South Indian

Servings   : 2

Ingredients

For cooking rice

½ cup rice (short to medium grained) or basmati rice or 3 cups cooked rice

¾ to 1 cups water - for pressure cooking

⅛ teaspoon salt or add as required

Other ingredients

½ cup grated carrots or 2 medium carrots grated or 100 grams carrots

½ teaspoon mustard seeds

1 small tej patta (Indian bay leaf)

½ inch cinnamon

1 to 2 green cardamoms

2 cloves

½ teaspoon chopped green chili or serrano pepper or 1 green chilli

5 to 6 curry leaves (medium-sized)

1 pinch asafoetida (hing) - optional

1.5 tablespoons oil - any neutral flavored oil

salt as required

<u>For garnish</u>

¼ cup sliced onions (tightly packed) or 1 small onion

10 to 12 cashews - kept whole or halved

10 to 12 raisins (without seeds)

1 to 2 tablespoons chopped coriander leaves (cilantro)

Instructions

<u>Cooking rice</u>

Soak rice in a bowl in enough water for 30 minutes. Drain and then set aside.

You could use any rice like sona masuri, surti kolam or parimal rice or even basmati rice. I used hand pounded sona masuri rice.

Add the rice in a 2 litre pressure cooker along with 0.75 to 1 cups water and salt (optional). Pressure cook for 2 whistles.

Since this rice was hand pounded rice, I cooked for 3 whistles and added 1.25 cups of water.

You can also cook the rice in a pot or pan adding 3 to 3.5 cups of water. Then drain the water once the rice grains are cooked.

When the rice is cooking, peel and grate 2 medium sized carrots. Keep the grated carrots aside. Also slice 1 small onion and chop one green chili.

When the pressure settles down on its own, open the lid of the cooker.

Gently fluff the rice grains and allow them to cool completely. I cooled the rice in the cooker itself. But you can also take the rice grains in a large plate or tray to cool them.

Sautéing

In a pan heat the oil and add the thinly sliced onions.

Stir and saute the onions on a low to medium heat until onions start to turn light golden. Add a pinch of salt for cooking the onions quickly.

When the onions begin to get light golden, add the cashews and raisins. Mix very well.

Sauté until the raisins become plump. By the time the raisins become plump, the onions will also get golden.

Remove the onions, cashews and raisins with a slotted spoon and keep aside.

Making carrot rice

In the same pan, some oil will be left. Lower the heat. Now add mustard seeds, tej patta, cinnamon, cardamoms and cloves.

Stir and sauté until the mustard crackles.

Now add the chopped green chilies, curry leaves and a pinch of asafetida (optional).

Stir and saute for half a minute. Add the grated carrots. Mix very well.

Saute the carrots for about 3 minutes on a low to medium heat. Depending on the size of gratings, the sautéing can take less or more time.

Add the steamed rice and stir. Season with salt. Again mix very well and switch off the flame.

Lastly add the fried onions, cashews and raisins. Also add chopped coriander leaves.

Mix very well. You can also garnish carrot rice with the fried onions, cashews and raisins while serving.

Serve carrot rice with a side raita or salad.

<u>**Serving suggestions**</u>

Serve carrot rice with a side of a raita or salad. You can even pack it as a tiffin box lunch with some chutney or a veggie stir fry.

The tangy sour flavors of an onion-tomato salad combine nicely with the mild, sweet flavors of this carrot rice.

In fact a tangy tomato salad or even a mayo salad will pair greatly. If you do not have any veggies, simply serve carrot rice with a simple plain curd (yogurt).

<u>**Storage**</u>

Though you mostly won't have any leftovers, but in case if you do have, then refrigerate and consume within a day. Do not keep for a longer time in the fridge. Rice is best had when freshly made.

<u>**Notes**</u>

<u>**Ingredients swaps**</u>

<u>**Rice**</u>: You could use any Indian variety of non-sticky rice to make this recipe. I make carrot rice with Indian varieties of rice but any non-indian varieties or strains of rice would also work well. Just that you will need to adjust the water and cooking time.

<u>**Oil**</u>: Neutral flavored oils are a better option for this recipe. But even coconut oil works nicely.

<u>**Onions**</u>: A variety of onions like shallots, pearl onions, scallions, red, white, and yellow onions can be added.

<u>**Dry fruits and nuts**</u>: If you do not have cashews or raisins, simply skip them or add the nuts that you have.

<u>**Spices**</u>: Though you can skip mustard seeds, but do include cinnamon, cloves, and green cardamoms. Instead of mustard seeds, you can also add cumin. Cumin would give a different flavor profile to the dish but will taste good. Curry leaves and asafetida can be omitted.

<u>**Green chillies**</u>: A bit of heat balances the sweetness in the carrot rice recipe.

So you can swap green chili peppers for any hot pepper of your choice. Simply add about ½ teaspoon of it. Or swap for ¼ teaspoon cayenne pepper or red chilli powder.

Recipe notes

Using leftover rice: If you have leftover steamed or cooked plain white rice - then you need only 3 cups of it. Simply follow all the recipe steps from sautéing the onions, spices, carrots, and mixing rice with the sautéed mixture.

Cooking rice in a pan: You can easily cook rice in a pan. Add the rice, salt, and 3 to 3.5 cups water in a pan. Simmer on medium-low heat until the rice grains are fluffy and tender. Drain the extra water. Let the cooked rice grains cool at room temperature.

Spicing: For small kids, you can skip the green chilies. If you like spicy food, then you can definitely add more green chilies or couple it with red chili powder or cayenne pepper. You can even add ¼ teaspoon of turmeric powder for yellow-colored rice. If you do not have whole spices like cinnamon, cardamom, and cloves, substituting about ¼ teaspoon garam masala powder will work too.

Veggies: Apart from carrots, some bell peppers (capsicum), cabbage, and steamed green peas or boiled corn kernels when added will make it a hearty meal.

Gluten-free recipe: To make this carrot rice gluten-free, skip the asafetida or use a gluten-free asafoetida.

Scaling: You could easily make a large batch of this carrot rice recipe.

Mushroom Pulao

This is a mild, flavorful mushroom pulao recipe made with coconut milk.

Prep Time   :   25 mins

Cook Time   :   25 mins

Total Time   :   50 mins

Cuisine   :   Goan

Servings   :   3

<u>Ingredients</u>

<u>main ingredients</u>

1.5 cups basmati rice – you can use any type of long grained rice

200 to 250 grams white button mushrooms, sliced or chopped

85 grams onion or 1 medium size onion, thinly sliced or finely chopped, about ⅓ to ½ cup sliced or chopped onions

1 medium size tomato or ⅓ cup chopped tomatoes

1 medium size potato, peeled & cubed (optional)

1 to 2 green chilies, chopped

½ tablespoon Ginger-Garlic Paste or 1 inch ginger + 6 to 7 garlic, crushed in mortar-pestle

1 cup thick coconut milk + 1.5 to 1.75 cups water or an overall of 2.5 to 2.75 cups water (add depending on the quality of rice. Usually most basmati rice which has been soaked for 20 to 30 mins before, requires about 2.5 cups of water if you want separate grains. for a slightly more cooked texture, you can add 2.75 to 3 cups of water)

2 tablespoons oil

salt or sea salt as required

<u>whole spices for mushroom pulao</u>

1 teaspoon cumin seeds , optional

3 green cardamoms

4 to 5 cloves

6 to 7 black pepper

1 to 1.5 inches cinnamon

Instructions

preparation for mushroom pulao

Clean, wash and soak the rice for 20 to 30 minutes.

When the rice is getting soaked, chop all the veggies. Rinse and chop the mushrooms too.

Take all the whole garam masala and keep it aside.

making mushroom pulao

In a pressure cooker, heat oil. Add the whole garam masala including cumin, and fry till they become fragrant. About a few seconds.

Add the onions and fry them till translucent.

Add the ginger-garlic paste and saute till the raw smell of the paste disappears.

Now add the chopped tomatoes, potatoes and mushrooms. Saute for 8-10 minutes till the mushrooms are half cooked. Keep on stirring in between.

Add the soaked rice and the chopped green chili.

Saute the rice for 1-2 minutes stirring in between on a low flame.

Add the coconut milk and water. Stir and season with salt.

Pressure cook mushroom pulao for 2 to 3 whistles.

When the pressure settles down on its own, remove the lid and gently fluff the rice.

Garnish with coriander leaves or mint leaves and serve mushroom pulao with sliced onions and lime. You could also have it with onion-tomato raita.

Paneer Fried Rice

Indian inspired delicious recipe of a mildly spiced paneer fried rice with mixed veggies, spices and herbs.

Prep Time   : 40 mins

Cook Time   : 15 mins

Total Time   : 55 mins

Cuisine   : Indian

Servings   : 3 to 4

Ingredients

for cooking rice

1 cup heaped rice, regular or basmati rice, 220 grams, or 4.5 to 5 cups leftover cooked rice

1.75 cups water

½ teaspoon oil

¼ teaspoon salt

other ingredients

2 tablespoon oil

½ teaspoon shahjeera (caraway seeds) or cumin seeds

1 medium onion chopped or 1/3 cup chopped onion

1 teaspoon Ginger-Garlic Paste or 3 to 4 garlic +½ inch ginger - crushed to a paste in mortar-pestle

1 medium to large tomato - chopped or ½ cup chopped tomatoes

1 small to medium carrot - grated or shredded or chopped finely, about 1/3

cup shredded carrots

7 to 9 french beans - thinly sliced or finely chopped, about 1/3 cup thinly sliced french beans

1 small bell pepper (capsicum) - finely chopped, about 1/3 cup finely chopped capsicum

250 grams Paneer (cottage cheese) - chopped in cubes

½ teaspoon crushed black pepper or pepper powder

¼ teaspoon red chili powder or add as per taste

½ teaspoon Garam Masala Powder

salt as required

Instructions

cooking rice

Rinse 1 heaped cup regular rice or basmati rice very well in water. Then soak the rice grains in water for 30 minutes.

After 30 minutes, drain and add the rice in a pressure cooker. Add salt.

Pour 1.75 cups of water and drizzle 1/2 tsp oil.

Stir and pressure cook the rice for 2 whistles or for about 10 minutes. When the pressure settles down on its own, remove the lid and fluff the rice. You can also cook the rice in a pot. If using cooked rice, the amount to be added is 4.5 to 5 cups of cooked rice.

You can also take the rice in a plate and Allow the grains to cool completely, Before you add them to the stir fried veggies.

prepping veggies

Meanwhile, when the rice is soaking, you can do the prep work by grating or shredding the carrot, thinly slicing the french beans, finely chopping the capsicum/green bell pepper and chopping the onion and tomato.

making paneer fried rice

Heat 2 tbsp oil in a deep pan or kadai and add ½ tsp shahjeera/caraway seeds or cumin seeds/jeera. Saute till they splutter.

Then add the finely chopped onions and saute till they turn translucent.

Add 1 tsp ginger-garlic paste and saute till the raw aroma of ginger-garlic goes away.

Next add the chopped tomatoes. Stir well. Saute till the tomatoes soften and turn mushy.

Now add the thinly sliced french beans. Stir fry on a medium flame for 3 to 4 minutes.

Then add the grated carrots and finely chopped capsicum. Mix and continue to stir fry on a medium flame for 4 to 5 minutes.

Then add paneer cubes. Also sprinkle some 1/2 tsp crushed black pepper or pepper powder, 1/4 tsp red chili powder and 1/2 tsp garam masala powder. Stir and mix very well.

Then add the cooked rice. Season with salt as required.

Gently stir and mix everything very well. You can add the rice in parts if you want.

Check the taste and add more spice powders or salt as per your taste preferences.

Serve paneer fried rice hot or warm with a side veggie salad or raita. I usually serve this dish with raita varieties like onion raita or boondi raita or cucumber raita. However the dish will taste good even without any accompaniment.

Notes

The recipe can be doubled or tripled.

You can use any variety of capsicum (bell pepper) - yellow, green or red.

Paneer can be replaced with tofu.

The amount of spices can be varied as per your taste preferences.

Mango Rice

This mango rice recipe is a spiced, tempered and tangy rice dish made from raw mangoes.

Prep Time   :   25 mins

Cook Time :   15 mins

Total Time   :   40 mins

Cuisines   :   Indian, Karnataka

Servings   :   4

Ingredients

for pressure cooking rice

1.5 cups regular rice

½ teaspoon salt

½ teaspoon oil

2.5 cups water

for the paste

½ cup grated coconut

1.5 cups peeled and chopped raw unripe mango or 250 grams raw mangoes - chopped

3 to 4 dry red chilies - broken and deseeded

1 green chili - chopped

1 teaspoon white sesame seeds

2 teaspoon peanuts

1 teaspoon jaggery - optional

other ingredients for mango rice

3 tablespoon peanut oil or sesame oil or any oil

1 or 2 dry red chilies - broken and deseeded

1 teaspoon mustard seeds

1 teaspoon chana dal (optional)

1 teaspoon urad dal (optional)

3 to 4 tablespoon peanuts

1 pinch asafoetida (hing)

¼ teaspoon turmeric powder

1 sprig curry leaves or 12 to 15 curry leaves

salt as required

Instructions

cooking rice

First soak 1.5 cups of rice in water for 20 minutes. Use any regular rice.

After 20 minutes, pressure cook the rice with 2.5 cups water, 1/2 tsp salt, 1/2 tsp oil for 2 whistles on high flame.

You can also cook the rice in a pot. If cooking in a pot, then you may need to add more water.

When the pressure settles down on its own, spread the rice on a plate.

Keep aside and allow the rice to cool at room temperature. When the rice is warm, cover and keep so that the rice grains do not dry out.

When the rice is cooking, rinse, peel and chop 1 large green mango. 250 grams mangoes or 1.5 cups chopped raw mango. Proportion is important here, so if you don't know the weight of the mangoes, then use the cup measurement.

making paste for mango rice

In a grinder jar, add the chopped mangoes along with 3 to 4 dry red chilies (broken and deseeded), 1 green chili (chopped), 1 tsp sesame seeds, 2 tsp peanuts, ½ cup grated coconut and 1 tsp powdered or grated jaggery.

I added jaggery to balance the sourness of the mangoes. If you don't have dry red chilies, then add green chilies. Add about 2 to 3 green chilies overall.

I used byadgi red chilies which are not very hot. If using a hotter variety of red chilies, reduce the amount to 1 or 2.

Without adding any water, grind to a semi-fine paste. Don't make a fine paste. Keep aside.

making mango rice

In a pan, heat 3 tbsp oil and add 3 to 4 tbsp peanuts.

On a low flame, saute the peanuts till they change color.

Then bring them to the side of the pan and add 1 tsp mustard seeds. Let the mustard seeds crackle.

You can also add 1 tsp each of chana dal and urad dal at this step. If adding chana dal or urad dal, allow them to turn golden before you proceed to the next step.

When the mustard seeds crackle add 12 to 15 curry leaves and 1 or 2 dry red chili. Stir and saute till the red chilies change color.

Then add a pinch of asafoetida, 1/4 tsp turmeric powder. Stir well.

Now add the ground raw mango-coconut-spices paste. Stir and saute for 3 to 4 minutes. Then season with salt.

Stir very well again. Remove from the stovetop and keep aside. To the cooked rice you can add the raw mango coconut masala.

You can mix in batches or at once. The rice has to be at room temperature before you start mixing.

Now with your hands gently mix the rice with the raw mango coconut masala. I mixed both the cooked rice and the masala in batches in a bowl.

Serve mango rice with some fried papads or chips.

You can also serve with some yogurt or a pickle. While serving mango rice, you can also garnish with chopped coriander leaves if you want.

Methi Pulao | Methi Rice

Easy, healthy and tasty one-pot methi pulao or methi rice made with fenugreek leaves, basmati rice, mix vegetables and spices.

Prep Time   :   30 mins

Cook Time   :   15 mins

Total Time   :   45 mins

Cuisine   :   Indian

Servings   :   4

Ingredients

Main ingredients

1 cup basmati rice or 200 grams basmati rice

2 cups methi leaves (fenugreek leaves) or 80 grams methi leaves, finely chopped

1 cup chopped mix vegetables - I added ½ cup chopped carrots and ½ cup green peas

1 medium to large onion, sliced or ½ cup thinly sliced onions

1 inch ginger + 3 to 4 garlic + 2 to 3 green chilies - crushed to a paste in mortar-pestle

¼ teaspoon turmeric powder (ground turmeric)

½ teaspoon red chili powder (cayenne pepper or paprika)

½ teaspoon coriander powder (ground coriander)

2 cups water

2 to 3 tablespoon oil

salt as required

Whole spices

½ teaspoon cumin seeds

1 black cardamom

2 green cardamoms

1 inch cinnamon

3 to 4 cloves

1 or 2 single strand of mace - optional

Instructions

Preparation

Rinse basmati rice in fresh water for 2 to 3 times.

Then soak rice in enough water for 30 minutes. After 30 minutes drain all the water and set the soaked rice aside.

When the rice is soaking, rinse and chop the methi leaves and other veggies.

Crush ginger, garlic and green chilies in a mortar-pestle. You can also grind them in a small chutney grinder.

Sautéing onions and fenugreek leaves

Heat in a 2 or 3 litre pressure cooker and fry the following spices until they splutter and are fragrant - cumin seeds, cardamom, green cardamoms, cinnamon, cloves and single strand of mace (optional).

Then add thinly sliced onions. Stir often and sauté the onions until they start turning golden.

Then add the crushed ginger+garlic+green chilli paste. Stir and saute for a few seconds until the raw aroma of ginger and garlic goes away.

Now add the finely chopped methi leaves. Stir and sauté for 3 to 4 minutes on a low to medium heat.

Then add chopped mix vegetables and mix well. You can add veggies of your choice.

Add turmeric powder, red chili powder and coriander powder. Mix very well again.

Making methi rice

Add the soaked basmati rice. Stir and saute for a minute.

Pour water. Season with salt as required and mix. You can also make the methi rice in a pan or pot. Add 2 to 2.5 cups of water if making in a pan.

Pressure cook on medium to high flame for 2 to 3 whistles or 8 to 9 minutes. When the pressure settles down on its own, remove the lid. Gently fluff the rice.

Serve methi pulao hot with plain curd or raita. I served aloo raita.

Serving suggestions

With raita: Serve methi rice with plain curd or raita. Methi pulao will pair nicely with most raita varieties like onion raita, cucumber raita, boondi raita or onion tomato raita.

With Dal: Even with a simple dal fry or dal tadka, methi pulao tastes delicious.

In a lunch box: Methi rice also stays good in the lunch box for some hours. When packing it in a lunch box, add a side of veggie salad or a mango or lemon pickle. You can also pack it for short travels.

Storing

I do not recommend freezing or making a large batch for freezing. Cooked rice is better fresh on the same day. If you have any leftovers then store in the fridge for a day only and not more than a day. Before serving, steam in a pan or Instant pot for 5 minutes.

Notes

Scaling: The recipe can be doubled or tripled to feed a large crowd.

Veggies: You can add vegetables of your choice or can make it without veggies. The veggies that make a perfect combination with fenugreek leaves in this pulao are - cauliflower, capsicum (bell pepper), corn, eggplant, broccoli, cabbage, button mushrooms, carrots and green peas.

Spices: Make a non-spicy methi pulao, by simply skipping the ground spices and green chillies.

Protein: Adding some tofu or paneer makes for a flavorful protein rich pulao. Lightly pan fry them and mix with the prepared methi rice before serving. Cooked chickpeas or canned chickpeas also make a nice addition.

Whole spices: If you do not have all the whole spices as listed in the recipe, then add whatever spices you have.

Rice: A short grained rice or even brown rice works well in the recipe. Simply add water as required with the kind of rice you have used.

Capsicum Rice

This Bell Pepper Rice is an easy, quick and delicious one pot recipe.

Prep Time   : 30 mins

Cook Time   : 15 mins

Total Time   : 45 mins

Cuisine   : North Indian

Servings   : 2 to 3

Ingredients

1 cup basmati rice or 200 grams basmati rice

2 tablespoon oil

1 teaspoon cumin seeds (jeera)

2 green cardamoms (choti elaichi)

2 cloves (lavang)

½ inch cinnamon (dalchini)

2 small tejpatta or 1 medium to large tejpatta (indian bay leaf)

2 single strands of mace (javitri)

1 medium onion, sliced or ½ cup sliced onions

75 to 80 grams capsicum or 2 medium capsicum or ¾ cup sliced capsicum (shimla mirch or bell pepper)

3 tablespoon chopped coriander leaves (dhania patta)

4 to 5 drops of lemon juice

1.75 cups water

salt as required

Instructions

preparation for capsicum rice

Rinse 1 cup basmati rice very well in water.

Then soak rice in water for 30 minutes. Later drain and keep the rice aside.

Meanwhile when the rice is soaking, slice the onions thinly. Also slice the capsicum.

<u>making capsicum rice</u>

Heat 2 tbsp oil in a pressure cooker. Add the whole spices - cumin seeds, green cardamoms, cloves, inch cinnamon, tejpatta, strands of mace.

Saute till the spices crackle and become fragrant.

Then add the sliced onions.

Stir very well and saute till the onions become golden.

Now add the sliced capsicum and chopped coriander leaves.

Stir very well and saute for 3 to 4 minutes.

Add the rice. Stir and saute for a minute.

Pour water and season with salt. Also add 3 to 4 drops of lemon juice. Stir.

Cover the pressure cooker with its lid and pressure cook capsicum rice on a medium to high flame for 2 to 3 whistles.

When the pressure falls down on its own, open the lid and gently fluff the capsicum rice.

Serve capsicum rice hot with some curry dish or a dal.

Pudina Rice

Pudina rice is a fragrant, spicy and tasty dish made with mint leaves and some more spices-herbs.

Prep Time   :   30 mins

Cook Time   :   15 mins

Total Time   :   45 mins

Cuisine   : Indian

Servings   : 3 to 4

Ingredients

for the mint paste

1 cup mint leaves, chopped,

½ cup coriander leaves, chopped (cilantro leaves)

1 to 2 green chillies, chopped

½ inch ginger, chopped or ½ teaspoon chopped ginger

3-4 garlic, chopped or ½ teaspoon chopped garlic

1 tablespoon chopped coconut or 2 tbsp grated coconut or 2 tbsp coconut milk (you can also add 2 tbsp desiccated coconut if you don't have fresh coconut)

1 teaspoon coriander seeds

½ teaspoon cumin seeds

2 to 3 tablespoon water for grinding or add as required

other ingredients

1 cup basmati rice or 200 grams basmati rice

2 cloves

2 small cardamom

1 inch piece of cinnamon

1 small to medium tej patta (indian bay leaf)

1 medium onion, thinly sliced

1 small tomato, sliced (optional)

1 small to medium potato, peeled and chopped

¼ cup heaped fresh or frozen peas

1.5 to 2 cups water

salt as required

Instructions

preparation

Rinse the 1 cup basmati rice (240 grams) till the water runs clear of the starch. Soak the rice in water for 30 minutes.

After 30 minutes, drain the rice and keep aside.

Meanwhile, when the rice is soaking, prep the other ingredients.

Take 1 cup chopped mint leaves, ½ cup chopped coriander leaves, ½ tsp chopped ginger, ½ tsp chopped garlic, 1 or 2 chopped green chilies, 1 tbsp chopped coconut or 2 tbsp coconut milk or grated coconut, 1 tsp coriander seeds, ½ tsp cumin seeds in a chutney grinder or small wet grinder.

Add 2 to 3 tbsp water and grind to a smooth paste. Add more water if required while grinding.

making pudina rice

Heat 2 tbsp oil in the pressure cooker.

Add the following whole spices - 1 inch cinnamon, 1 tej patta, 2 green cardamoms, 3 cloves, 2 to 3 single strands of mace and a small piece of stone flower (stone flower is optional).

Fry the spices for some seconds till they become aromatic.

Then add sliced onions. About 1 medium onion which has been thinly sliced.

Saute till the onions become golden. Then add the ground mint paste.

Add ¼ tsp turmeric powder and ¼ tsp red chili powder. Stir and saute the masala paste for a minute or two.

Then add chopped potatoes, tomatoes and green peas. About 1 small to medium potato, chopped, 1 small tomato, chopped and ¼ cup fresh or frozen peas. Stir.

Add the drained rice and stir gently. The oil should coat the rice grains well. Stir & saute for a minute.

<u>cooking pudina rice</u>

Add 1.5 to 2 cups of water. Stir well.

I added 2 cups since I had used organic basmati rice and we prefer the rice grains to be cooked well. 1.5 cups will give an al dente texture and can be added for the regular indian brands of basmati rice.

Add salt. Stir again.

Cover the lid tightly and pressure cook mint rice for 2 to 3 whistles till the rice grains are cooked.

When the pressure settles down on its own, open the lid and gently fluff the rice.

Serve pudina rice hot with plain curd or with onion-tomato raita or boondi raita.

Kashmiri Pulao

Kashmiri pulao is aromatic, mild and faintly sweet in taste.

Prep Time   :   30 mins

Cook Time   :   15 mins

Total Time   :   45 mins

Cuisine   :   Indian, Kashmiri

Servings   :   3 to 4

<u>Ingredients</u>

<u>**for kashmiri pulao**</u>

1 cup basmati rice soaked in water for 30 minutes

1 inch cinnamon

1 teaspoon caraway seeds (shahjeera)

1 tej patta (indian bay leaf)

3 cloves

2 to 3 green cardamoms

2 black cardamoms

½ teaspoon dry ginger powder (saunth)

1 teaspoon fennel powder

2 pinches of saffron

2 tablespoon oil or ghee (clarified butter)

4 to 4.25 cups water

salt as required

<u>**for garnishing kashmiri pulao**</u>

1 medium sized onion, sliced thinly

10 to 12 cashews

10 to 12 almonds

10 tp 12 walnuts

2 tablespoon oil or ghee

Instructions

<u>**making kashmiri pulao**</u>

On a low or medium flame, heat oil or ghee in a deep pan.

Add 1 inch cinnamon stick, 1 teaspoon caraway seeds, 1 bay leaf, 3 cloves, 2 to 3 green cardamoms and 2 black cardamoms.

Fry the spices till the oil becomes fragrant.

Now lower the flame. Add the ½ teaspoon dry ginger powder (saunth) and 1 teaspoon fennel powder (saunf powder). stir well.

Add 1 cup of soaked and drained basmati rice and stir.

Add 2 pinches of crushed saffron (kesar). saute for a minute.

Pour 2 cups of water and salt as required. Stir and cover the pan tightly. When the rice is cooking, prepare the garnish.

garnishing kashmiri pulao

Heat 2 tbsp oil in a frying pan. Add the sliced onions.

Also add a pinch of salt and fry the onions till they are golden or caramelized and crisp. Remove and drain on paper tissues.

In the same oil, first fry the 10 to 12 almonds till they become crisp. Remove and drain fried almonds on paper tissues.

Now fry 10 to 12 cashews till they are crisp and lightly browned. drain them on paper tissues.

Also fry 10 to 12 walnuts till they are crisp and lightly browned. remove fried walnuts. Drain them on paper tissues.

Cook the rice till all the water is absorbed and the rice is cooked. When done, fluff the rice.

While serving the kashmiri pulao, garnish with the fried onions and dry fruits.

Serve kashmiri pulao hot with raita or salad.

Yakhni Pulao with Vegetables

This is a vegetarian version of fragrant yakhni pulao from Hyderabadi cuisine.

Prep Time : 20 mins

Cook Time : 20 mins

Total Time : 40 mins

Cuisine : Hyderabadi

Servings : 4

<u>Ingredients</u>

<u>for the bouquet garni</u>

1 tablespoon coriander seeds

1 teaspoon cumin seeds

½ tablespoon fennel seeds

1 inch ginger + 5 to 6 small to medium garlic cloves, crushed

<u>for vegetable yakhni</u>

1.5 cups chopped veggies like cauliflower, carrots, french beans, peas

½ cup green peas, fresh or frozen

5 cups water

salt as required

<u>for yakhni pulao</u>

2 tablespoons ghee

1 cup basmati rice, soaked in water for 30 minutes

2 to 3 small tej patta

1 medium sized onion, thinly sliced or ⅓ cup sliced onions

3 green cardamoms

1 inch cinnamon

1 black cardamom

4 to 5 black peppers

3 cloves

3 tablespoons Curd (yogurt)

salt as required

for the garnish

1 small sized onion, thinly sliced or or ⅓ cup sliced onions

2 tablespoons chopped coriander or mint leaves

12 to 15 cashews (optional)

1 tablespoon ghee

Instructions

making bouquet garni

Take coriander seeds, fennel seeds, cumin seeds and crushed ginger+garlic in a muslin cloth.

Tie the muslin cloth securely with the spices inside it. This is the bouquet garni.

making vegetable yakhni (veg stock)

Heat 5 cups of water. Add 1.5 cup mixed chopped veggies, green peas and salt as required.

Also place the bouquet garni in the pan along with the veggies. Cook the veggies till they are half done.

Squeeze the bouquet garni and discard the spices.

Through a strainer strain the stock/yakhni and keep the veggies aside.

Strain and take 2 cups of stock. remaining veg stock can be added to any soup, dal or gravy dish.

making vegetable yakhni pulao

Rinse 1 cup basmati rice. Then soak the basmati rice in water for 30 minutes.

Heat 2 tablespoons ghee in a pan.

Add the other whole spices - cloves, cinnamon, cardamom, bay leaves, black cardamom and peppercorns. Fry till they are fragrant.

Add sliced onion. Fry the onion till they are browned.

Add the soaked and drained basmati rice. Stir the basmati rice well.

Now add the half cooked veggies and 2 to 2.25 cups of the broth (yakhni). Add salt if required. We have already added salt to the yakhni. Keep this in mind before adding the salt.

Add curd (yogurt). Mix well.

Cover with a tight lid. I have wrapped the lid with a cotton cloth or kitchen napkin to cook the pulao on dum.

Cook for 15 to 20 minutes on a low flame.

Later open the pan. If the rice appears not to be completely cooked and the mixture looks dry, just add some warm yakhni/broth to the rice. Gently stir with a fork. Cover tightly and cook for a few minutes more.

If there is some stock in the pulao, then do not add any extra veg stock. Just cover the pan and cook further for some more minutes.

garnishing yakhni pulao

Take one tablespoon ghee or oil in a pan. Add ⅓ cup thinly sliced onions.

Once the onion changes to a light brown color. You can add some cashews and fry with the onion. fry till the onion becomes golden brown.

Garnish the pulao with fried onions and fried cashew nuts and some chopped coriander or mint leaves.

Serve veg yakhni pulao hot with onion raita or with onion mint kachumber.

Jeera Rice

Give a makeover to the simple steamed rice by adding cumin (jeera) and some fragrant spices. This restaurant style cumin rice recipe is mildly spiced, fragrant and tastes too good. Recipe post shares two methods of making jeera rice. Choose the recipe method that suits you.

Prep Time   : 30 mins

Cook Time   : 25 mins

Total Time   : 55 mins

Cuisine   : North Indian

Servings   : 4

<u>Ingredients</u>

<u>for cooking rice</u>

1 cup basmati rice

4 cups water

1 tej patta (indian bay leaf)

2 green cardamoms

1 black cardamom

½ inch cinnamon

2 cloves

1 to 2 single strands of mace

1 teaspoon salt or as required

for tempering jeera rice

2 tablespoons oil or 1.5 tablespoon ghee (clarified butter)

2 teaspoons cumin seeds

1 green chilli - chopped, optional

1 tablespoon chopped coriander leaves

(cilantro leaves)

Instructions

cooking rice

Rinse basmati rice till the water runs clear of starch. Soak the rice for 30 mins and then drain all the water. Keep aside.

Heat 4 cups of water till it comes to a boil. Add all the whole spices. Add rice and salt. Simmer the rice on a low flame uncovered.

The rice grains should be cooked till tender and yet separate. Drain the water and keep the cooked rice aside.

If you want you can rinse the rice with water at room temperature. This stops the cooking of the rice and keeps the grains separate.

making jeera rice

Heat oil in a small pan. Add cumin/jeera.

Let them crackle. They have to be fried well otherwise you will taste uncooked cumin in the rice.

Add the green chilies. Stir for a few seconds. No need to brown the chilies.

Add the tempering to the hot or warm rice.

With a fork, gently mix the tempering with the rice grains. Even if some rice grains break, it's alright. Do gently take care so as not to break the rice grains.

Add coriander and gently mix or garnish the rice with coriander at the time of serving.

Serve jeera rice hot or warm with a dal or vegetable/paneer curry of your choice.

Notes

If using leftover rice, then you will need about 3 cups of cooked rice to use the same proportion of ingredients as mentioned in the recipe.

Chana Pulao

Chana pulao is an aromatic pulao made with white chickpeas (garbanzo beans or kabuli chana)

Prep Time   : 20 mins

Cook Time   : 30 mins

Total Time   : 50 mins

Cuisine   : North Indian

Servings   : 3 to 4

Ingredients

main ingredients

¾ cup white chickpeas (safed chana or kabuli chana or chole)

1 cup heaped basmati rice, 200 grams rice

1 medium to large onion, sliced thinly

1 medium tomato, chopped

¼ teaspoon red chili powder

1 pinch Garam Masala Powder

1 pinch turmeric powder

1 pinch saffron strands - optional,

½ teaspoon lemon or lime juice or 1 teaspoon yogurt (curd)

2 tablespoon ghee or oil

1.75 cups water for pressure cooking the rice

a few chopped mint leaves for garnish (or coriander leaves)

salt as required

whole spices

½ teaspoon caraway seeds

1 black cardamom

2 small green cardamom

2 single thin strand of mace

1 tej patta (indian bay leaf)

2 to 3 cloves

1 inch cinnamon stick

for the green paste

¾ inch ginger, chopped

3 to 4 garlic, chopped

1 tablespoon mint leaves, chopped

3 tablespoon coriander leaves, chopped (cilantro leaves)

1 green chili, chopped

½ to 1 tablespoon water for grinding

Instructions

preparation

Rinse and soak white chickpeas (chana or chole) overnight or for 8 to 9 hours in enough water.

Drain them well.

Then add the drained chickpeas to the pressure cooker. Add 3 to 3.5 cups of water.

Also add about 1/2 tsp of salt and pressure cook for 12 to 14 whistles or more, till the chickpeas are tender and cooked well.

Drain the cooked chickpeas and keep aside.

Rinse the rice very well in water till the water runs clear of starch.

Then soak the rice in enough water for 30 mins. Strain and keep aside.

Make a smooth paste of the ingredients, mentioned under 'green paste' in a chutney grinder or magic bullet with very little water. Keep this green paste aside

Slice the onion and chop the tomato.

making chana pulao

In a pressure cooker heat ghee or oil and add all the whole spices – caraway seeds, cardamoms, mace, cinnamon, cloves, bay leaf.

Saute the whole garam masala or whole spices for some seconds till fragrant, and then add the sliced onions.

Saute the onions till golden brown.

Now add the green paste and saute till the raw aroma of the ginger-garlic goes away. Add the chopped tomatoes and saute for two minutes.

Next add the turmeric powder, red chili powder and garam masala powder.

Saute the tomatoes for a minute or so and add the basmati rice. Mix well and saute the entire mixture for a minute.

Add the drained cooked chana (chickpeas).

Add the curd or lemon juice, saffron threads and again mix everything well.

Now add 1.75 cups of water.

Season with salt and pressure cook the pulao for 2 to 3 whistles. I pressure cooked for 2 whistles.

When the pressure settles down on its own, then open the lid of the cooker.

Gently fluff the rice. Garnish with coriander leaves or mint leaves.

Serve chana pulao hot with raita, pickle, papad or any veg salad.

<u>Notes</u>

This chickpea rice recipe can also be made in a pot or pan.

Just add 2 cups of water to the rice in a deep pot or pan.

Cover and cook till the rice grains are done and all the water is absorbed.

Paneer Pulao

This is a fragrant and lightly spiced paneer pulao made with freshly ground pulao masala which really brings in a lot of flavor and aroma in the recipe.

Prep Time   :   30 mins

Cook Time   :   20 mins

Total Time   :   50 mins

Cuisine   :   Indian

Servings   :   4

Ingredients

for the pulao masala

½ teaspoon cumin seeds

½ teaspoon caraway seeds (shah jeera)

¼ teaspoon fennel seeds

1 black cardamom - seeds removed and husks discarded

2 to 3 green cardamom - kept whole or seeds removed

2 to 3 cloves

1 inch cinnamon

1 single strand of mace

a small piece of stone flower (rock flower or pathar phool or dagad phool or kalpasi)

for paneer pulao

1.5 cups basmati rice or pulao rice

250 to 300 grams Paneer (cottage cheese)

1 medium to large onion, thinly sliced

⅓ cup peas - optional

2 tablespoon ghee or oil for the pulao

2 to 3 teaspoon ghee or oil for pan frying the paneer

3 to 3.25 cups water

½ inch ginger + 2 to 3 garlic cloves + 1 green chilli - crushed in a mortar-pestle to a paste

1 tej patta (indian bay leaf)

1 to 1.25 teaspoon lemon juice

1.5 to 2 tablespoon chopped mint leaves

salt as required

Instructions

making the pulao masala

In a small dry grinder or coffee grinder, add all the spices mentioned: "For the pulao masala".

Grind to a semi fine to fine powder. Keep aside.

making pulao

Rinse the basmati rice till the water becomes clear of the starch.

Soaked the basmati rice in enough water for 30 minutes. After 30 minutes drain and keep the rice aside.

Slice the onions thinly. Chop the mint leaves and keep aside.

Crush the ginger, garlic and green chilli to a paste in a mortar-pestle.

Heat ghee in a pot or a pan. Add the bay leaf and saute for 2-3 seconds.

Then add the thinly sliced onions and saute till the onions start to turn golden brown or caramelize.

Then add the ginger, garlic and green chilli paste. Saute till the raw aroma of ginger garlic goes away. (on a low flame, it will take approx 10-15 seconds).

Add the chopped mint leaves and the ground pulao masala. Stir for 5-8 seconds.

Optional step - if you are adding peas then add now and saute for 2-3 minutes.

Add the drained rice. Stir gently and saute for a minute. Add water, lemon juice and salt.

Stir well. Cover the pan tightly with a lid. Make sure no steam escapes from the sides.

On a low to medium flame, simmer till the rice grains are cooked. If the water dries in the pan then add some more water.

<u>making paneer pulao</u>

When the rice is cooking, chop the paneer into cubes.

Heat ghee on a tawa or a frying pan. Use a non-stick pan or a well seasoned tawa/griddle to pan fry the paneer. Otherwise the paneer cubes will stick to the pan.

Add the paneer cubes and pan fry till light golden. Don't over fry as then they will become dense and rubbery. Keep the pan fried paneer cubes aside.

Once the rice is cooked, just allow the rice to sit for 5 minutes.

Then add the pan fried paneer cubes and gently mix it with the rice.

Cover the pan again with a lid and allow the paneer to be in the rice for another 5 minutes.

This makes the paneer soft and it also absorbs the aroma of the pulao.

Serve paneer pulao hot garnished with some mint leaves and pan fried paneer cubes.

You can serve raita or dal fry or dal tadka with the paneer pulao.

<u>Notes</u>

For pressure cooking paneer pulao:

Add 2.5 cups water for separate grains and for a more soft texture of rice, add 3 cups water.

Pressure cook pulao for 2 to 3 whistles.

Mushroom Fried Rice

Mushroom fried rice is a stir fried Chinese style fried rice with mushrooms.

Prep Time   : 20 mins

Cook Time   : 10 mins

Total Time   :   30 mins

Cuisine   : Indo Chinese

Servings   :   2

Ingredients

1 heaped cup basmati rice or long grained rice

5 cups water for cooking rice

200 to 250 grams white button mushrooms

3 small to medium garlic cloves, finely chopped

1 medium onion or 2 to 3 small to medium spring onions, chopped finely

½ tablespoon chopped celery

1 tablespoon naturally fermented soy sauce

3 tablespoon oil

salt and black pepper as required

Instructions

cooking rice

First rinse the rice till the water runs clear of the starch.

Then cook the rice in 5 cups of water with a few drops of oil and some salt.

The rice should be cooked al dente or just cooked.

Don't cook the rice till it becomes mushy or too soft. Drain the rice in a colander and keep aside.

After the initial steam passes from the rice, cover the colander with a lid.

Let the rice cool completely before you add it to the mushrooms.

<u>making mushroom fried rice</u>

Heat oil in a wok or kadai. Add the garlic and onions first and stir fry for 2 mins on a high flame.

Then add the chopped mushrooms and stir fry for 5-6 mins or more on a high flame till the mushrooms begin to get lightly browned from the edges.

First the whole mixture will become watery as mushrooms will release water and slowly slowly the water will evaporate and you will see oil floating in the mixture.

When the mushrooms start to become lightly browned, then add the celery and stir fry for a minute.

Add soy sauce, black pepper and salt.

Stir and then add the rice. Stir gently but briskly. Stir fry for 2-3 minutes.

Serve the mushroom fried rice hot garnished with celery or spring onion greens with a side indo chinese vegetable dish like veg balls in hot garlic sauce, sweet and sour vegetables, veg manchurian.

<u>Notes</u>

To give some heat in the dish, you can add a bit of red chili powder or cayenne pepper.

Substitute fresh coriander/cilantro leaves if you do not have celery.

For a gluten free mushroom fried rice recipe you can use tamari instead of soy sauce.

I have used button mushrooms in this recipe. However, you can make it with shiitake mushrooms or cremini mushrooms or use a combination of various varieties of edible mushrooms.

You can use any neutral-flavored oil. Even toasted sesame oil tastes very good.

Spinach rice (palak rice) Recipes

This is a very simple one pot recipe of spinach rice. Spinach with all its health benefits makes a good combo with veggies, lentils and cereals.

Prep Time   : 15 mins

Cook Time   : 15 mins

Total Time   : 30 mins

Cuisine   : North Indian

Servings   : 3 to 4

<u>Ingredients</u>

for spinach puree

3 cups roughly chopped spinach (palak) or 1 cup spinach puree

1 to 3 green chilies - chopped

½ inch ginger - chopped

3 to 4 garlic cloves - chopped

other ingredients for spinach rice

2 tablespoon oil

1 tej patta or indian bay leaf

3 to 4 cloves

½ inch cinnamon

2 green cardamoms

1 mace strand

1 small star anise

1 teaspoon cumin seeds

50 grams onion or 1 medium onion thinly sliced or ⅓ cup sliced onions

2 to 3 drops of lemon juice, optional

1 to 1.25 cups water

salt as required

Instructions

preparation for spinach rice

Rinse 1 cup basmati rice till the water runs clear of starch. Then soak the rice grains in enough water for 30 minutes. Later drain and keep aside.

When the rice is soaking, rinse the spinach leaves very well and chop them. You will need 3 cups of roughly chopped spinach.

Now add the spinach leaves in a blender or grinder jar. Also add 1 to 3 green chilies, 1/2 inch ginger and 3 to 4 garlic cloves (all chopped).

Blend to a smooth puree. Keep covered aside.

making spinach rice

In a pressure cooker, heat 2 tbsp oil.

Add the following spices and saute them till they splutter - 1 tej patta or indian bay leaf, 3 to 4 cloves, 1/2 inch cinnamon, 2 green cardamoms, 1 mace strand, 1 small star anise and 1 tsp cumin seeds.

Next add 1/3 cup thinly sliced onions. Stir and saute the onions till light golden or golden.

Add the spinach puree. Stir and saute for 4 to 5 minutes on a low flame.

Add the rice and mix rice very well.

Add salt and water. 1 cup water gives al dente rice. For a softer texture in the rice you can add 1.25 cups of water. I added 1.25 cups of water.

Stir very well. At this step you can also add a few drops of lemon juice.

Cover and pressure cook spinach rice for 8 to 9 minutes or 2 to 3 whistles.

When the pressure falls down in the cooker on its own, then remove the lid and gently fluff the rice.

Serve palak rice hot with a side salad or pickle or raita. While serving, if you want you can garnish with some chopped coriander or mint leaves.

Notes

For making the spinach rice in a pot or pan, add water accordingly.

Chana Biryani

Chana biryani is an aromatic, spiced and a delicious dum cooked and layered biryani made with white chickpeas.

Prep Time   : 45 mins

Cook Time   : 30 mins

Total Time   : 1 hr 15 mins

Cuisine   : Hyderabadi, South Indian

Servings   : 3 to 4

Ingredients

for chana gravy

2 to 3 tablespoon oil

1 teaspoon caraway seeds (shah jeera)

2 to 3 green cardamoms

1 black cardamom

1.5 inch cinnamon

1 tej patta (indian bay leaf)

2 to 3 cloves

2 large onions or 160 grams onions or 1 cup tightly packed thinly sliced onions

1 large tomato or 100 grams tomatoes or ½ cup chopped tomatoes

5 grams ginger or 1 inch ginger or ½ tablespoon finely chopped ginger

5 gram garlic or 8-10 medium sized garlic cloves, or ½ tablespoon finely chopped garlic

2-3 green chilies, slit or sliced diagonally

¾ to 1 cup coconut milk or 200 to 250 ml coconut milk

½ teaspoon turmeric powder

½ teaspoon red chilli powder

1 teaspoon coriander powder (ground coriander)

1 cup white chickpeas (chole or chana) or 200 grams chana, soaked overnight in enough water

2.25 cup water for pressure cooking chana gravy

salt as required

for rice

200 grams basmati rice or 1 cup heaped basmati rice

3 cups water for cooking rice

2 to 3 green cardamoms

1 black cardamom

1 to 1.5 inch cinnamon (dalchini)

2 to 3 single strands of mace

1 tej patta (indian bay leaf)

3 cloves

½ teaspoon salt or add as required

<u>for layering biryani</u>

10 grams mint leaves or ½ cup chopped mint leaves

10 grams coriander leaves or ½ cup chopped coriander leaves

2 teaspoon ginger julienne

1 tablespoon warm water + 1 pinch of saffron strands

1 to 2 teaspoon kewra water or rose water

Instructions

<u>preparation</u>

Rinse and then soak 1 cup of safed chane or dry white chickpeas (200 grams) in enough water overnight or for 8 to 9 hours. Later strain, rinse the chickpeas and keep aside.

Soak 1 cup heaped basmati rice in enough water for 30 minutes. Later strain the rice and keep aside.

Heat 3 cups of water in a pan or pot. When the water becomes hot, add the following spices - 2 to 3 green cardamoms, 1 black cardamom, 1 to 1.5 inch cinnamon, 2 to 3 single strands of mace, 1 tej patta and 3 cloves.

Add 1/2 tsp salt or as required.

Bring the water to a rolling boil on a high flame.

Then add the strained rice.

Cook the rice grains on the high flame.

When the rice grains are 75% cooked or there is a slight bite in them, then switch off the flame.

Immediately strain the cooked rice. Keep aside.

making chana gravy for biryani

So when the rice grains are getting soaked and cooking, you can prepare the chana gravy.

Heat 2 tbsp oil and add these spices - 1 tsp shah jeera, 2 to 3 green cardamoms, 1 black cardamom, 1.5 inch cinnamon/dalchini, 1 tej patta and 2 to 3 cloves/lavang.

Saute the spices for a few seconds till they splutter.

Then add the 1 cup tightly packed thinly sliced onions. Stir very well.

Saute the onions on a low to medium flame.

For a quick cooking of the onions, add a pinch of salt.

Saute till the onions become golden.

Switch off the flame and take half of the fried onions on a plate.

Add 1/2 tbsp finely chopped ginger, 1/2 tbsp finely chopped garlic and 2 to 3 green chilies (sliced).

Switch on the burner and saute for some seconds till the raw aroma of ginger-garlic goes away.

Then add 1/2 cup chopped tomatoes and saute for a minute.

Next add 1/2 tsp turmeric powder, 1/2 tsp red chilli powder and 1 tsp coriander powder.

Mix the spice powders very well with the rest of the ingredients.

Add the soaked and drained chana.

Mix the chana very well with the rest of the masala.

Add 2.25 cups of water. season with salt.

Pressure cook the chickpeas on a medium to high flame for 18 to 20 minutes.

When the pressure falls down on its own, remove the lid and check the chickpeas. They should be cooked well and softened.

Do note that the chickpeas should not have a bite to them. If not cooked well, then pressure cook for a few more whistles. The time taken to cook chickpeas, depends on their quality, so cook accordingly.

Then add 3/4 to 1 cup thick coconut milk (200 to 250 ml). Stir and mix very well. Check the salt in the chana gravy and if required add more.

When the chickpeas are cooking, warm 1 tbsp water and add a pinch of saffron strands. Stir and keep aside. You can also use milk instead of water.

assembling and making chana biryani

Add 1/4 cup chopped coriander leaves, 1/4 cup chopped mint leaves and 1 tsp ginger julienne to the chana gravy.

Layer with all of the rice.

Next top with the fried onions.

Then layer with 1/4 cup chopped coriander leaves, 1/4 cup chopped mint leaves and 1 tsp ginger julienne.

Sprinkle the saffron dissolved water evenly.

Now place a moist kitchen towel on the pressure cooker.

Place a tight lid. Keep the cooker on a heated tawa/griddle.

Dum cook the biryani for 25 to 30 minutes on a low flame. Give a resting time of 5 to 7 minutes.

Later serve chole biryani with a raita, salad or biryani shorba.

Notes

Tips for making chana biryani:

Coconut milk can be substituted with 1 cup fresh curd.

Substitute caraway seeds with cumin seeds.

Dry fruits like cashews, almonds and raisins can also be added.

Ghee can be used instead of oil.

Bengali Khichdi

Bhaja muger dal khichuri is one pot meal of rice, moong dal, vegetables that is made during durga puja.

Prep Time   :   30 mins

Cook Time   : 15 mins

Total Time   :   45 mins

Cuisine   :   Bengali, Indian

Servings   :   3 to 4

Ingredients

1 cup basmati rice or govind bhog rice (basmati chawal ya govind bhog chawal)

1 cup dhuli moong dal (split and husked moong dal)

3 tablespoon ghee or 2.5 tablespoon oil

1 inch cinnamon

2 green cardamom

3 cloves

1 tej patta (indian bay leaf)

1 teaspoon cumin seeds or cumin powder

1 inch grated ginger

½ teaspoon turmeric powder

½ to ¾ teaspoon red chili powder

1 pinch asafoetida (hing) - optional

2 small tomatoes, chopped (optional)

1 green chili, chopped

2 small to medium potatoes, ½ cup cauliflower and ½ cup green peas or 1 to 1.5 cups of chopped mix vegetables like cauliflower, peas, potatoes and carrots

½ teaspoon sugar or as required - optional

rock salt (edible and food grade) or sendha namak as required

5 cups water

Instructions

preparation

Rinse and soak rice in water for 30 mins.

In a pan slow roast the moong dal till some of the lentils turn light golden and aromatic.

Keep on stirring to get uniform roasting and browning.

When the lentils cool, rinse them in water. Sprinkle some water on them and keep aside.

Just before you begin tempering, drain both the moong dal as well as rice and keep aside.

<u>**making khichuri**</u>

Heat ghee or oil in the pressure cooker.

First fry the whole spices till they become aromatic - cinnamon, cardamom, cloves, bay leaf and cumin.

The cumin should also crackle when frying the spices.

Now add the grated ginger and saute for 5-6 seconds or till the raw aroma of the ginger goes away.

Add turmeric, red chili powder and asafoetida and saute for 2-3 seconds.

Then add the tomatoes and green chilies and saute till the tomatoes become soft.

Add the chopped veggies - potato, cauliflower and peas.

Stir and saute for a minute.

Add the roasted moong dal and saute for 2 minutes.

Add the drained rice and stir well.

Pour 5 cups of water and add salt & sugar.

Stir and then pressure cook khichuri for 4-5 whistles on medium to high flame.

Once the pressure settles down on its own, open the lid of the cooker.

Serve the khichuri with baingan bhaja or yogurt and some roasted papads by the side.

Notes

To get a porridge like consistency in the khichdi you can add an additional ½ to 1 cup water.

Spinach (Palak) Khichdi

Palak khichdi is a sumptuous and nutritious khichdi made with mung lentils, rice, spinach and peanuts.

Prep Time   : 30 mins

Cook Time : 10 mins

Total Time : 40 mins

Cuisine   : Indian

Servings   : 3 to 4

Ingredients

2 cups chopped palak (spinach)

¼ or ⅓ cup raw peanuts

½ cup moong dal (yellow mung lentils)

½ cup long grained rice or basmati rice

1 medium size onion, finely chopped

1 medium size tomato, chopped

1 medium size potato, chopped

1 inch cinnamon

1 tej patta (indian bay leaf)

2 cloves

2 green cardamoms

½ teaspoon caraway seeds (shah jeera) or cumin seeds

½ inch ginger + 3 to 4 garlic - crushed in a mortar-pestle to a paste or 1 teaspoon ginger garlic paste

1 green chilli, chopped

¼ teaspoon turmeric powder

1 pinch asafoetida (hing) * check notes

salt as required

2 tablespoon ghee or oil

3.5 to 4 cups water

Instructions

preparation

Pick and rinse both the rice and moong dal together.

Soak them together in enough water for about 30 minutes.

Rinse the palak or spinach leaves well.

Chop them and then in a mixer or blender, make a smooth puree of the spinach adding very little water. Keep the spinach puree aside.

making palak khichdi

Heat ghee or oil in the pressure cooker. Add the caraway seeds or cumin seeds, cinnamon, bay leaf, cloves and cardamoms.

Fry the whole spices for some seconds till they become fragrant. Add the finely chopped onion and saute till they become golden.

Add the ginger-garlic paste and the chopped green chilies. Saute for about 15-20 seconds or till the raw aroma of the ginger-garlic goes away.

Then add the chopped tomatoes and saute till they begin to soften.

Add the turmeric powder and asafoetida and stir well.

Now add the peanuts, potatoes and saute for about 2 minutes.

Add the spinach puree and continue to saute for 2-3 minutes.

Strain the rice and moong dal and add them to the spinach mixture. Stir well.

<u>**cooking palak khichdi**</u>

Pour 3.5 to 4 cups of water. Add salt and stir well.

Check the taste and if required add some more salt. Pressure cook the khichdi on medium flame for 5 to 6 whistles.

Once the pressure settles down on its own, remove the lid. Check the consistency of the khichdi.

If the khichdi looks thick, then you can add some hot water and simmer for a few minutes.

Remember to stir often as otherwise the khichdi gets stuck at the bottom. If the khichdi appears thin, then simmer till you get the desired consistency.

While serving, pour the palak khichdi in bowls or plates and top with 1/2 to 1 tsp of ghee.

Serve hot with plain curd/yogurt or raita or a simple vegetable salad.

Notes

Skip the asafoetida for a gluten free version of this khichdi.

Chana Dal Khichdi

This is a simple and flavorful traditional Punjabi chana dal khichdi made with basmati rice, bengal gram and spices.

Prep Time   : 30 mins

Cook Time : 20 mins

Total Time : 50 mins

Cuisine   : North Indian, Punjabi

Servings   : 2 to 3

Ingredients

½ cup basmati rice or broken basmati or regular rice

½ cup chana dal (spilt-skinned bengal gram)

1 pinch asafoetida (hing)

1 to 2 pinch red chili powder

1 cup water

1 tablespoon oil

salt as required

Instructions

soaking chana dal

First rinse and soak the chana dal overnight or for 4-5 hours or soak for 30 minutes in hot water. Also rinse and soak the rice for 30 minutes. Later, strain the chana dal of the water and keep aside.

cooking chana dal

Heat oil in the pressure cooker. Lower the flame. Add the red chili powder, asafoetida and salt.

Stir and fry for a few seconds. Add the chana dal. Stir and then add 1 cup water.

Cover the pressure cooker with its lid and pressure cook for 1 or 2 whistles or for about 6 minutes. Once the pressure settles down on its own, remove the lid.

The dal should be cooked and also should be separate.

You can also cook the dal for 1 whistle and then check. If not cooked then cook for 1 more whistle. Remember the dal should not be mushy.

making punjabi chana dal khichdi

Drain the rice and add the rice to the cooked dal in the pressure cooker.

There will be water in the cooker along with the cooked dal, so no need to add extra water.

Stir and again pressure cook for 1 or 2 whistles. The dal would cook further more along with the rice.

Once the pressure settles down on its own, remove the lid.

The specialty of this khichdi is the separate grains of rice and dal and it is not mushy nor pasty. If the rice is not cooked, then you can add about ⅛ to ¼ cup water and pressure cook again for a whistle or two.

Serve the punjabi chana dal khichdi steaming hot with yogurt or raita variety like onion raita or onion tomato raita. You can also serve lemon pickle or mango pickle with it.

This khichdi tastes best when it is eaten hot. It does not taste so good when it cools down. That's why I won't suggest packing it for lunch or tiffin box as this khichdi becomes dry as it cools.

Notes

The recipe can be doubled or tripled.

Rajma Pulao

Aromatic spiced rice pulao made with kidney beans, herbs and spices.

Prep Time   : 9 hrs

Cook Time   : 35 mins

Total Time   : 9 hrs 35 mins

Cuisine   : North Indian

Servings   : 2 to 3

Ingredients

for cooking rajma

½ cup rajma (kidney beans) or 90 to 100 grams rajma

2 cups water for pressure cooking

¼ teaspoon salt (optional)

whole spices

1 small to medium tej patta (indian bay leaf)

3 cloves

2 to 3 green cardamoms

1 black cardamom

½ inch cinnamon

½ teaspoon cumin seeds - shah jeera also can be added instead of cumin seeds

to be crushed to a paste

1 inch ginger or 8 grams ginger

6 to 7 garlic cloves or 7 to 8 grams garlic cloves

1 or 2 green chilies, chopped

other ingredients

3 tablespoon oil

1 medium onion, thinly sliced or ⅓ cup thinly sliced onions or 60 grams onion, thinly sliced

¼ cup chopped coriander leaves (cilantro leaves)

¼ teaspoon turmeric powder (ground turmeric)

½ teaspoon red chili powder

½ teaspoon coriander powder (ground coriander)

1 cup heaped basmati rice or 200 grams basmati rice, soaked in enough water for 30 minutes

1.75 to 2 cups water (do add water depending on the quality of basmati rice)

½ teaspoon lemon juice

salt as required

1 to 2 tablespoon chopped coriander leaves for garnish (cilantro leaves)

Instructions

cooking rajma

A night before or for 8 to 9 hours, rinse ½ cup rajma a couple of times and then soak in water.

The next day, discard the soaked water. Then rinse the rajma beans again very well in running water. Drain.

Add the rinsed rajma to a pressure cooker along with 2 cups of water. You can also add ¼ tsp salt if you want.

Pressure cook for 15 to 20 whistles or for 12 to 17 minutes. First I cooked rajma beans for 15 whistles and found that the beans were still uncooked from the center. So I pressure cooked for 5 whistles more.

Rajma has to be cooked very well. There should be no redness or bite in the rajma. Pressure cooking time will vary depending on the quality of rajma.

When the pressure settles down in the cooker, then remove the lid. Strain the rajma. Keep aside.

soaking rice

Before you keep the rajma for cooking, rinse 1 heaped cup basmati rice very well in water till the water runs clear of starch.

Then soak the rice in enough water for 30 minutes. After 30 minutes strain the rice off all the water and keep aside.

preparing ginger+garlic+green chili paste

In a mortar-pestle take 1 inch ginger (roughly chopped), 6 to 7 garlic cloves (roughly chopped) and 1 or 2 green chilies, chopped.

Crush to a coarse paste. You can also use a small grinder to make this paste. Keep aside.

Thinly slice one medium onion. Also chop coriander leaves and keep aside.

making rajma pulao

Just rinse the same pressure cooker in which we cooked rajma beans, with water and then keep again on the stove top. Add 3 tbsp oil.

When the oil becomes hot, lower the flame and add these whole spices - 1 small to medium tej patta, 3 cloves, 2 to 3 green cardamoms, 1 black cardamom, ½ inch cinnamon and ½ tsp cumin seeds.

Let the spices crackle.

Now add 1/3 cup thinly sliced onions. On a low to medium flame, begin sauteing the onions. Saute the onions till they start to become golden.

Now add the crushed ginger+garlic+green chilli paste along with ¼ cup chopped coriander leaves.

Stir and saute till the raw aroma of ginger-garlic goes away. This takes a few seconds.

Add the cooked rajma beans.

Next add ¼ tsp turmeric powder, ½ tsp red chili powder and ½ tsp coriander powder. Mix well.

Add the rice. Season with salt.

Gently stir and mix the rice and salt with the rest of the ingredients.

cooking rajma pulao

Now add 2 cups of water. You can add 1.75 cups to 2 cups of water. Do add water depending on the quality of basmati rice.

Lastly add ½ tsp lemon juice.

Cover and pressure cook the pulao on a medium to high flame for 2 to 3 whistles or 8 to 9 minutes.

When the pressure comes down on its own, open the lid and gently fluff the pulao.

Garnish with some chopped coriander leaves and serve rajma pulao hot with your favorite raita or salad or pickle.

<u>Notes</u>

- for cooking kidney beans in a pot or pan:Take a deep bottomed pan or pot. Add 2.5 to 3 cups of water along with the kidney beans. Cover the pan and on a medium to high flame cook the beans. If required add more hot water.- for cooking pulao in a pot.Add 2 cups water. On a low to medium flame, cover and cook till rice is done.

Coconut Milk Rice

Coconut milk rice is a mild, fragrant rice dish made with coconut milk and mixed veggies.

Prep Time   :   20 mins

Cook Time   : 20 mins

Total Time   : 40 mins

Cuisine   :   South Indian

Servings   :   2 to 3

<u>Ingredients</u>

1 cup basmati rice or 200 grams basmati rice

1 medium to large onion, thinly sliced or 1 cup thinly sliced onions

½ inch ginger + 2 to 3 garlic + 1 green chili - crushed to a paste in mortar-pestle

½ cup green peas + 1/3 cup chopped french beans or 3/4 cup of any mixed chopped veggies - fresh or frozen

5 to 6 curry leaves or 1 medium sized tej patta (indian bay leaf)

3 to 4 cloves

3 to 4 green cardamoms

1 inch cinnamon

1 single strand of mace

½ teaspoon cumin seeds

¾ cup thick coconut milk or about 200 ml thick coconut milk

1 to 1.25 cups water

2 tablespoon oil

few chopped coriander leaves (cilantro leaves) or mint leaves for garnish

salt as required

Instructions

preparation

Rinse basmati rice very well in water till the water runs clear of the starch. Soak the rice in enough water for 20 minutes. After 20 minutes, drain the rice and keep aside.

When the rice is soaking, prep up the veggies by chopping them. Slice the onions thinly. Also crush 1/2 inch ginger + 2 to 3 garlic + 1 green chili in a mortar-pestle.

making coconut milk rice

Heat 2 tbsp oil in a pressure cooker and add the whole spices - 3 to 4 cloves, 3 to 4 green cardamoms, 1 inch cinnamon, 1 single strand of mace and 1/2 tsp cumin seeds. Saute the spices till they splutter and become fragrant.

Now add 1 cup thinly sliced onions and 5 to 6 curry leaves. If you do not have curry leaves, then add 1 medium sized tej patta/indian bay leaf when you saute the whole spices. Stir very well.

Saute till the onions turn translucent or a light golden.

Then add the crushed ginger+garlic+green chilies paste. Stir and saute till the raw aroma of ginger and garlic goes away.

Now add 10 to 12 cashews, which have been chopped. Cashews are optional and you can skip them. Stir again.

Now add the mixed veggies. You can add 3/4 cup of any mixed veggies. I added 1/2 cup green peas and 1/3 cup chopped french beans.

Stir and saute the veggies for a minute.

Then add the rice grains.

Gently mix and stir the rice grains with the rest of the ingredients.

cooking coconut milk rice

Now pour 3/4 cup thick coconut milk. You can also add 1 cup thick coconut milk.

Add 1 to 1.25 cups water. Stir well. If using 1 cup coconut milk, then add 0.75 to 1 cup water.

Then season with salt. Taste the stock and it should feel slightly salty.

Cover and pressure cook for 1 to 2 whistles or for 8 to 9 minutes. I pressure cooked for 2 whistles.

When the pressure settles down naturally, open the lid and gently fluff the rice.

Garnish with some chopped coriander or mint leaves. Serve coconut milk rice with a side dish of raita, biryani shorba gravy or some pickle and salad.

Beetroot Rice

This beetroot rice is slightly spicy with the sweetness of beetroot coming through in the spiced rice.

Prep Time   : 20 mins

Cook Time : 15 mins

Total Time   :   35 mins

Cuisine   : South Indian

Servings   :   3 to 4

Ingredients

prepping rice

1 cup basmati rice or 200 grams basmati rice

enough water for soaking rice

whole spices

2 tablespoon oil

2 to 3 green cardamoms

1 inch cinnamon

2 to 3 cloves

5 to 6 black pepper

½ teaspoon mustard seeds

½ teaspoon cumin seeds

remaining ingredients

1 medium onion chopped or 1/3 cup chopped onion or 50 to 55 grams onions

7 to 8 curry leaves or 1 small to medium tej patta (indian bay leaf)

2 small to medium beetroots or 1 cup finely chopped beets or 125 grams beetroots

1 teaspoon Ginger-Garlic Paste or ½ inch ginger + 3 to 4 small to medium garlic cloves

1 green chili, chopped

¼ cup chopped coriander leaves (cilantro leaves)

¼ teaspoon turmeric powder (ground turmeric)

¼ teaspoon red chili powder (or cayenne pepper or paprika)

½ teaspoon coriander powder (ground coriander)

1.5 to 2 cups water, i added 1.5 cups water

salt as required

2 tablespoon chopped coriander leaves for garnish (cilantro leaves)

Instructions

prepping rice

Rinse basmati rice in water very well. Then soak the rice in enough water for 20 minutes.

After 20 minutes, drain the rice and keep aside. Instead of basmati rice, you can even use any other fragrant rice or even regular or short grained rice.

making beetroot rice

Heat 2 tbsp oil in a pressure cooker. Then add all the whole spices.

The oil should be hot enough so that the mustard seeds crackle as soon as you add them in the oil. Do keep the flame on a low to medium flame, so that the other spices do not get burnt.

Add ⅓ cup chopped onion and 7 to 8 curry leaves.

Stir and saute till the onion starts to become light golden.

Then add 1 tsp ginger-garlic paste, 1 to 2 green chilies (slit) and ¼ cup chopped coriander leaves.

Saute for a few seconds till the raw aroma of ginger-garlic goes away.

Now add 1 cup finely chopped beetroot. Do chop the beetroot finely. You can also grate beetroots and then add. Stir and saute for a minute.

Add ¼ tsp turmeric powder, ¼ tsp red chili powder and ½ tsp coriander powder. Mix and stir well. Add the rice.

Stir gently and saute for a minute.

cooking beetroot rice

Add 1.5 to 2 cups of water. Depending on the type and quality of rice, you can add water. For basmati rice, you can add 1.5 to 1.75 cups of water. I added 1.5 cups of water.

Season with salt as required. Stir and mix. Taste the water and it should have a slightly salty taste.

Pressure cook on a medium flame for 2 whistles or for 8 to 9 minutes. You can also cook this pulao in a pan or pot. If cooking in a pan then add the water accordingly. It will take more time to cook in a pot but you can do it.

When the pressure settles down on its own, remove the lid. Gently fluff the rice.

Garnish with 2 tbsp chopped coriander leaves. Serve beetroot rice with a side veggie salad or raita. It will go well with any raita variety like boondi raita or cucumber raita or onion raita.

Notes

The recipe can be doubled or tripled.

The amount of spices can be altered as per your taste.

If you want to add some more vegetables to this recipe, then I suggest adding green peas, potatoes and carrots. In greens, you can add a small amount of fenugreek or spinach leaves.

Jaggery Rice

Sweet-tasting traditional Punjabi rice dish made using jaggery, rice and spices.

Prep Time   :   45 mins

Cook Time   :   5 mins

Total Time   :   50 mins

Cuisine   :   Pakistani

Servings   :   2 to 3

<u>Ingredients</u>

<u>main ingredients</u>

¾ cup rice, preferably basmati rice

1 to 1.5 tablespoon oil

¾ cups water

4 small cardamoms

4 cloves

15 to 20 raisins

1 tej patta (indian bay leaf) - optional

1 tablespoon roasted peanuts - optional

<u>for soaking jaggery</u>

120 grams jaggery

¾ cup water

Instructions

First, take the jaggery and soak it in 3/4 cup water for 30 to 45 minutes.

Pick, clean and wash the rice. Soak the rice for 15 to 20 minutes.

In a pressure cooker add the rice and 3/4 cup water.

Pressure cook for 2 to 3 minutes. The rice should be half cooked. Once the pressure settles down, open the cooker lid.

Fluff the rice in the cooker itself.

Add the jaggery dissolved in water plus the oil. Stir it gently with the half cooked rice.

Now add the cardamom, cloves, bay leaf, raisins and peanuts.

Stir this too gently with the rice mixture.

Now close the cooker with the lid and pressure cook again for 2 to 3 minutes.

Garnish the cooked jaggery rice with dry fruits of your choice.

Serve hot or warm, plain or with some milk.

Lobia pulao

Pulao made with black eyed beans, onions, herbs and spices.

Prep Time   :   15 mins

Cook Time   :   15 mins

Total Time   :   30 mins

Cuisine   :   North Indian

Servings   :   2 to 3

Ingredients

for pressure cooking lobia

½ cup lobia (black eyed beans or chawli or rongi) or 120 grams lobia

1.5 cups water for pressure cooking

¼ teaspoon salt

for cooking pulao

2 tablespoon oil (can use sunflower or safflower or peanut oil)

½ teaspoon cumin seeds (jeera)

½ inch cinnamon (dalchini)

3 to 4 cloves (lavang)

2 to 3 green cardamom (choti elaichi)

1 small to medium tej patta (indian bay leaf)

90 to 100 grams onions or 2 medium onions or ¾ cup sliced onions

½ teaspoon Ginger-Garlic Paste or ½ inch ginger and 3 to 4 medium garlic cloves - crushed in mortar-pestle

2 medium tomatoes, chopped or ¾ cup chopped tomatoes

1 green chili, chopped

¼ teaspoon turmeric powder (haldi)

½ teaspoon red chilli powder (lal mirch powder)

½ teaspoon coriander powder (dhania powder)

1 tablespoons chopped coriander leaves (dhania patta)

1 cup heaped basmati rice or 200 grams basmati rice

1.75 cups water

salt as required

2 tablespoons chopped coriander leaves for garnish

Instructions

cooking the lobia beans

Rinse the lobia beans a couple of times in water. Then add them in a pressure cooker along with 1/4 teaspoon salt.

Pour 1.5 cups of water. Cover and pressure cook lobia on a medium flame for 7 to 8 minutes or for about 9 to 10 whistles. The cooking time varies with the quality and freshness of the lobia beans.

This variety of lobia beans were taking a long time to cook. First I pressure cooked for 5 whistles and then checked them. They were still uncooked. Then I again pressure cooked for 5 whistles.

The lobia beans should be cooked well, but not become mushy.

Strain the beans and keep aside.

When the lobia beans are cooking, rinse 1 heaped cup basmati rice in water till the water runs clear of starch. Then soak them for 30 minutes in enough water. After 30 minutes, drain the water and keep aside.

making lobia pulao

Use the same pressure cooker. Just rinse and use again or you can use another pressure cooker.

Heat 2 tablespoons of oil in it. Then add the whole spices - 1/2 teaspoon cumin seeds, 1/2 inch cinnamon, 3 to 4 cloves, 2 to 3 green cardamoms and 1 small to medium tej patta.

When the spices splutter and become aromatic, add 3/4 cup thinly sliced onions.

Saute the onions stirring often on a low to medium flame, till they begin to get golden brown.

Then add 1/2 teaspoon ginger garlic paste. Stir and saute till the aroma of ginger-garlic goes away.

Now add ¾ cup chopped tomatoes and 1 green chili (chopped). Mix well and saute for a minute.

Next add 1/4 teaspoon turmeric powder, 1/2 teaspoon red chilli powder and 1/2 teaspoon coriander powder. Mix well.

Add 1 tablespoons chopped coriander leaves. Stir well.

cooking lobia pulao

Then add the cooked lobia beans. Mix the beans with the onion-tomato masala mixture.

Now add the rice. Stir and mix the rice with the rest of the ingredients.

Pour 1.75 cups of water. Season with salt. Stir. Check the taste of water and it should be slightly salty. Stir.

On a medium flame, cover and pressure cook lobia pulao for 7 to 8 minutes or 2 to 3 whistles.

When the pressure in the cooker falls down on its own, remove the lid and gently fluff the rice.

Garnish with some coriander leaves and serve lobia pulao hot with a side of raita or veg salad.

Notes

- for cooking black eyed beans in a pot or pan:Rinse and soak the beans overnight or for at least 3 to 4 hours. Take a deep bottomed pan or pot. Add 2 to 2.5 cups of water along with the black eyed beans and salt. Cover the pan and on a medium to high flame cook the beans. If required add more hot water.- for cooking pulao in a pot.Saute the spices, onions etc in a thick bottomed pot. After adding soaked rice, add 2 cups of water. On a low to medium flame, cover and cook till rice is done and all the water is absorbed.

Wadi chawal

A delicious rice dish made with wadi which is spiced & sun-dried lentil dumplings.

Prep Time   :   5 mins

Cook Time   :   15 mins

Total Time   :   20 mins

Cuisine   :   Punjabi

Servings   :   3 to 4

Ingredients

1.5 cups rice

½ teaspoon cumin seeds

1 onion, chopped

1 teaspoon Ginger-Garlic Paste

2 tomatoes, chopped

1 green chili, chopped

½ teaspoon turmeric powder

½ teaspoon Garam Masala Powder

½ teaspoon red chili powder

8 to 10 wadis

3.5 cups water

2 tablespoon oil or ghee

salt as required

a few coriander leaves for garnishing

Instructions

Heat oil in a pan.

Splutter the cumin seeds.

Add chopped onion and then fry till golden.

Now add ginger-garlic paste and fry till the raw aroma disappears.

Add tomatoes and fry them till they become pulpy.

Now add all the dry spice powders plus green chilies and saute the whole masala till the oil separates.

Add the rice and mix well.

Rinse the wadis in water and add it to the rice. pour water.

Add salt and cover the pan. cook the rice till done.

Serve wadi chawal hot garnished with coriander leaves.

Notes

You can also make the wadi chawal in a pressure cooker. In this case just add 3 cups of water.

The recipe can also be made in ghee instead of oil.

Potato Rice

This potato pulao is a simple and minimally spiced rice dish made with potatoes.

Prep Time   :   30 mins

Cook Time   :   12 mins

Total Time   :   42 mins

Cuisine   :   South Indian

Servings   :   2 to 3

Ingredients

for soaking rice

1 cup heaped basmati rice

1.5 cups water for soaking rice

other ingredients

2 medium to large potatoes or 200 to 215 grams potatoes

2 tablespoon oil

1 tej patta (indian bay leaf)

2 green cardamoms

3 cloves

½ inch cinnamon

¼ teaspoon mustard seeds

1 medium onion or 50 grams onions or ⅓ cup thinly sliced onions

1 sprig curry leaves or 8 to 10 curry leaves

¼ teaspoon turmeric powder

1.5 to 1.75 cups water for pressure cooking

salt as required

1 to 2 tablespoon chopped coriander or mint leaves for garnish

to be ground to a paste

1 medium tomato or 60 grams tomatoes or ⅓ cup chopped tomatoes

3 to 4 garlic cloves - chopped

½ inch ginger - chopped

1 to 2 green chilies - chopped

¼ cup chopped coriander leaves or ¼ cup half-half of mint + coriander leaves

¼ teaspoon fennel seeds

¼ teaspoon cumin seeds

Instructions

preparation

Rinse 1 heaped cup basmati rice very well in water till the water runs clear of starch.

Then soak the rice in water for 30 minutes. Then later, drain all the water from the rice and keep aside.

In a chutney grinder jar or a small grinder jar, take the following ingredients - ⅓ cup chopped tomatoes, 3 to 4 small to medium garlic cloves (chopped), 1/2 inch ginger (chopped), 1 or 2 green chilies (chopped), 1/4 cup chopped coriander leaves, 1/4 teaspoon fennel seeds and 1/4 teaspoon cumin seeds.

Without adding any water, grind to a smooth paste. The juices from the tomato will help in grinding. Keep this masala paste aside.

making potato rice

Heat 2 tablespoon oil in a pan. Lower the flame and first add the whole spices - 1 tej patta, 2 green cardamoms, 3 cloves and 1/2 inch cinnamon.

Next add 1/4 teaspoon mustard seeds. Saute till the mustard seeds splutter.

Then add 1/3 cup thinly sliced onions. Saute the onions till they begin to get light brown.

Then add 8 to 10 curry leaves. Saute for 5 to 6 seconds.

Then add the ground masala paste. Mix very well and saute for a minute.

Add 1/4 teaspoon turmeric powder. Mix the turmeric powder very well with the rest of the masala.

Add chopped potatoes. Stir and mix the potatoes with the rest of the pulao masala.

Now add the rice. Stir and mix the rice evenly with the masala.

cooking potato rice

Add water. You can add 1.5 cups to 1.75 cups of water. Do add water depending on the quality of basmati rice. Stir very well.

Season with salt. Check the taste of the water and it should taste a bit salty.

Cover and pressure cook on a medium flame for 2 to 3 whistles or 6 to 7 minutes.

When the pressure comes down on its own, open the lid and gently fluff the rice.

Garnish with some coriander leaves or mint leaves while serving potato rice. Accompany a raita, salad or pickle by the side.

Notes

For cooking potato pulao in a pan or pot

Saute everything as mentioned in the recipe in a thick bottomed pan or pot.

Add soaked rice and then 1.75 cups water.

On a low to medium flame, cover and cook till all the water is absorbed and the rice is cooked. Depending on the quality of rice, you can add 2 cups of water too.

Kashmiri Biryani

Kashmiri biryani is a no onion no garlic biryani from the Kashmiri pandit cuisine.

Prep Time   :   40 mins

Cook Time   :   30 mins

Total Time   :   1 hr 10 mins

Cuisine   :   Indian, Kashmiri

Servings   :   5 to 6

Ingredients

<u>for rice</u>

1.25 cups basmati rice soaked for 30 mins

5 cups water to cook the rice

salt as required

1 pinch saffron

<u>for the veg curry</u>

½ cup chopped carrot

½ cup chopped cauliflower

½ cup green peas

½ cup chopped potato

3 tablespoons ghee (clarified butter) or oil

1 teaspoon caraway seeds

2 inch cinnamon

2 black cardamoms

3 to 4 green cardamoms

3 to 4 cloves

1 or 2 single strands of mace

1.5 teaspoon fennel powder

1 teaspoon dry ginger powder

½ or 1 teaspoon red chili powder

1 teaspoon Garam Masala Powder or kashmiri veri masala

¼ teaspoon asafoetida powder (hing)

¼ teaspoon grated nutmeg

5 to 6 tablespoon beaten fresh yogurt (curd) - dairy or cashew yogurt

1 cup water or add as required

salt as required

for the layers

2 tablespoons chopped mint leaves

2 tablespoons chopped coriander leaves (cilantro leaves)

2 pinches of saffron soaked in ⅔ cup warm water or warm milk or warm yogurt

for garnish

20 to 25 whole cashews or a mix of almonds, cashews and raisins - roasted or fried in some oil

a few mint leaves - optional

Instructions

cooking rice

Pick and rinse 1.25 cups of basmati rice in running water till the water runs clear of starch. Then soak the basmati rice in water for 30 minutes.

After 30 minutes drain the water and keep the rice aside. In a pot boil 5 cups of water and then add the soaked rice.

Cook the rice till they are ¾ cooked or 75% cooked. Then drain the rice in a colander. Sprinkle 1 pinch of saffron on the rice.

Keep the rice covered so that the rice does not dry out.

preparing veg gravy for biryani

Chop cauliflower, potatoes, carrots, mint leaves and coriander leaves. Also soak 2 pinches of saffron in ⅔ cup warm water or warm milk or warm yogurt.

Heat 3 tablespoons of ghee or oil in a pan or pressure cooker.

Add the following whole spices - 1 teaspoon caraway seeds, 2 inch cinnamon sticks, 2 black cardamom, 3 to 4 green cardamoms, 3 to 4 cloves and 1 to 2 strands of mace.

Fry till the spices splutter and become fragrant.

Now add ½ cup chopped cauliflower, ½ cup chopped carrots, ½ cup chopped potatoes and ½ cup green peas. Saute the veggies for 1 to 2 minutes.

Then add the following spice powders - 1.5 teaspoons fennel powder, 1 teaspoon ginger powder, ½ or 1 teaspoon red chili powder, 1 teaspoon garam masala powder or kashmiri veri masala, ¼ teaspoon asafoetida and ¼ teaspoon grated nutmeg. Saute for 2 minutes. Keep on stirring.

Keep the flame to a low and then add 5 to 6 tablespoons beaten fresh yogurt (curd or dahi) and stir well.

Add water and salt as required. Mix well.

Cover the pan with its lid and cook till the veggies are done. If there is too much water in the gravy then simmer till some water dries up. The gravy should be of medium or slightly thick consistency and should not be watery.

If using a pressure cooker, then pressure cook for 1 to 2 whistles till the veggies are cooked. Don't over cook the veggies.

assembling and layering kashmiri biryani

In a heavy thick bottomed pan, layer half of the gravy first.

Next layer half of the rice.

Sprinkle some of the chopped mint and coriander leaves.

Also sprinkle some of the saffron which was dissolved in warm milk or warm water or warm yogurt.

Now layer with the rest of vegetable curry.

Next layer with remaining rice.

Sprinkle the mint, coriander and saffron milk again.

cooking kashmiri biryani

Then cover the pan or pot with a tight fitting lid.

Take a tawa or griddle and heat it on medium flame. You can begin to preheat the tawa when you begin to assemble and layer the biryani.

When the tawa becomes hot, then lower the flame. Keep the sealed biryani pot on the tava. Keep the flame to the lowest and dum cook biryani for 25 to 30 minutes.

Alternatively, you can also dum cook the biryani for the first 15 minutes on direct low flame and then for the last 10 minutes, place the pot on the hot tava and cook on a low flame.

After 25 to 30 minutes, switch off the flame. Give a standing time of 5 to 7 minutes and then check the biryani. If there is still some liquid or water at the bottom then the biryani needs to be dum cooked for some more minutes. Cook till all the liquids are absorbed.

When the kashmiri biryani is getting dum cooked, you can roast 20 to 25 cashews or fry them in some oil or ghee. Alternatively you can also roast a mix of cashews, raisins and almonds or fry them in some oil.

While serving, garnish with the roasted or fried cashews, almonds and raisins along with some chopped mint leaves.

Serve the kashmiri biryani hot or warm along a raita by the side.

Notes

<u>Method to bake kashmiri biryani</u>

Preheat the oven at 180 degree celsius for 10 to 15 minutes.

When the oven is getting preheated then assemble the biryani as mentioned above in the oven proof utensil. Remember to use an oven proof glass utensils like the pyrex bowl or oven safe steel pan for baking in the oven.

Cover the bowl or pan with aluminium foil or the pyrex bowl lid and then bake biryani for 25 to 30 minutes. However the baking time will vary from oven to oven.

When done give a rest time of 5 to 7 minutes.

Then check the kashmiri biryani. If there is still some liquid or water at the bottom then the biryani needs to be baked for some more minutes till all the liquids are absorbed.

Tomato Biryani

One pot spiced South Indian style delicious tomato biryani.

Prep Time   :   30 mins

Cook Time   :   25 mins

Total Time   :   55 mins

Cuisine   :   South Indian

Servings   :   3

<u>Ingredients</u>

<u>main ingredients</u>

1 cup seeraga samba rice, 200 grams (can use basmati rice instead)

150 grams tomatoes or 2 large tomatoes or 1 cup chopped tomatoes or ½ cup tomato puree

2 tablespoon oil (sesame oil, peanut oil or sunflower oil)

35 grams onions or 1 small onion or ¼ cup thinly sliced onions

1 teaspoon Ginger-Garlic Paste

1 green chili, chopped

1 tablespoon chopped coriander leaves

1 tablespoon chopped mint leaves

¼ teaspoon turmeric powder

¼ teaspoon red chili powder

½ teaspoon coriander powder

¼ teaspoon Garam Masala Powder

1 inch medium potato chopped in small cubes

⅓ cup green peas , fresh or frozen

½ cup thick coconut milk

1.5 cups water or add as required

salt as required

whole spices

1.5 inches cinnamon

3 green cardamoms

3 cloves

1 small to medium sized tej patta

½ teaspoon cumin seeds

½ teaspoon fennel seeds

a small tiny piece of stone flower (pathar phool, dagad phool), optional

2 single strands of mace

Instructions

preparation

Rinse a couple of times and then soak 1 cup seeraga samba rice in water for 30 minutes. You can even use basmati rice or sona masuri rice.

After 30 minutes, drain the rice of all the water and keep aside.

Meanwhile, rinse and chop the tomatoes. Add them in a blender or grinder jar.

Blend to a smooth puree. If you do not have a blender or grinder, then you can even mince or grate the tomatoes.

Remove and keep the whole spices aside.

Slice one small onion thinly and keep aside. Also chop one green chili.

making tomato biryani

Heat 2 tablespoons oil in a thick bottomed pot or pan. Please do Use a thick bottomed pan, otherwise there are chances that the rice can get browned or burnt from the bottom.

Add all the whole spices and saute them till they crackle and turn fragrant.

Now add 1/4 cup sliced onions. Saute onions till they begin to get golden.

Add 1 teaspoon ginger garlic paste. Mix well.

Then add 1 tablespoon chopped coriander leaves, 1 tablespoon chopped mint leaves and 1 green chili (chopped). Mix well.

Add the tomato puree. If using ready tomato puree, then add 1/2 cup tomato puree. Mix again.

Now add 1/4 teaspoon turmeric powder, 1/4 teaspoon red chili powder, 1/2 teaspoon coriander powder, 1/4 teaspoon garam masala powder.

Mix the masalas very well with the mixture of tomato puree and other ingredients.

Stir and saute for 2 minutes.

Now add 3/4 to 1 cup of chopped veggies. I used green peas and potatoes. Mix again.

Add rice. Mix the rice with the rest of the tomato masala gravy.

Add 1.5 cups of water. then add 1/2 cup thick coconut milk and salt as per taste. Mix very well.

Cover the pan with a tight-fitting lid and cook the biryani on a slow flame for 18 to 20 minutes or until the rice is cooked and all the water is absorbed.

Once done, remove the lid. Then gently fluff the rice.

Serve tomato biryani hot with some pickle or raita of your choice.

Notes

If you do not have coconut milk, then just skip it and add water.

Coconut Rice

This is a light, mild South Indian coconut rice made with freshly grated coconut. It is also known as thengai sadam.

Prep Time   : 30 mins

Cook Time   : 10 mins

Total Time   :   40 mins

Cuisine   :   South Indian

Servings   :   3

Ingredients

for cooking rice

1 cup basmati rice or any regular rice or 4 to 4.5 cups cooked rice

1.75 to 2 cups water

for tempering

1.5 tablespoon coconut oil or any oil

1 teaspoon mustard seeds

½ tablespoon urad dal (split and husked black gram)

½ tablespoon chana dal (bengal gram)

10 to 12 cashews - chopped

1 or 2 dry red chilies

1 or 2 green chilies - chopped

1 pinch asafoetida (hing) - optional

10 to 12 curry leaves

1.5 cups tightly packed grated fresh coconut

salt as required

Instructions

preparation

Soak 1 cup regular rice or basmati rice in enough water for 30 minutes.

Also soak 1/2 tbsp urad dal and 1/2 tbsp chana dal in hot water for 30 minutes. Later drain the water very well and keep the dals aside. You can add the dals directly also, but soaking them and then adding gives a good taste to the coconut rice.

Grate half of a medium to large coconut and keep aside. You should be able to get about 1.5 cups tightly packed grated coconut.

cooking rice

After 30 minutes, drain the water and pressure cook the rice with 1.75 to 2 cups water for 2 whistles. When the pressure settles down on its own, open the lid and fluff the rice. For a softer texture in the rice, pressure cook for 3 whistles

Take the rice in a plate/tray and allow to cool grains completely. You can also cool the rice in the cooker itself. If there are lumps in the rice, then break the lumps once the rice is cooled.

making tempering for coconut rice

Heat 1.5 tbsp coconut oil in a pan. You can also use sesame oil or any other oil. Crackle 1 tsp mustard seeds.

Add the chana dal and urad dal. Stir and saute for about a minute.

Then add chopped cashews.

Stir and saute till the cashews turn golden. The dals would also turn golden by then.

Add 1 or 2 dry red chilies, 10 to 12 curry leaves and 1 or 2 chopped green chilies along with a pinch of asafoetida.

Stir and saute till the red chilies change color.

making coconut rice

Next add grated coconut. Stir very well.

Saute the coconut for 3 to 4 minutes. The coconut can be sauteed till a creamish color or a faint light brown color.

Lastly add the steamed rice and salt.

Stir the rice well and switch off the flame.

Serve coconut rice topped with a bit of ghee or some coriander leaves. Accompaniments can be cured, or kuzhambu or potato roast.

I served thengai sadam with a spiced south indian potato curry.

Kathal (jackfruit) Biryani

This raw unripe jackfruit biryani is a mildly spiced and subtly flavored meaty vegetarian biryani made with jackfruit or kathal.

Prep Time   :   45 mins

Cook Time   :   30 mins

Total Time   : 1 hr 15 mins

Cuisine   :   Indian

Servings   : 4 to 5

Ingredients

for the rice

1.5 cups basmati rice

4 cups water for cooking the rice

water for soaking the rice

one single strand of mace

2 green cardamoms

1 inch cinnamon

2 to 3 cloves

1 tejpatta (indian bay leaf)

salt as required

for jackfruit biryani gravy

300 to 350 grams raw unripe jackfruit or about 3 cup chopped jackfruit

(kathal)

1 cup full fat curd (yogurt)

½ teaspoon turmeric

½ teaspoon red chili powder

a single strand of mace

a small piece of stone flower (patthar ke phool or dagad phool or kalpasi)

3 green cardamoms

1 inch cinnamon

3 cloves

1 teaspoon shah jeera (caraway seeds)

2 medium to large onions, thinly sliced

1 medium tomato, chopped

1.5 tablespoon chopped coriander leaves

1.5 tablespoon chopped mint leaves

3 tablespoon ghee

1 inch ginger + 3 to 4 garlic cloves +1 green chili - crushed to a paste in a mortar pestle or in a small grinder or magic bullet.

1.5 to 2 cups water

salt as required

for layering jackfruit biryani

1 teaspoon ghee

3 tablespoon milk

2 pinch of saffron

1 teaspoon kewra water (pandan) or rose water

Instructions

preparing rice

First rinse the rice till the water runs clear of the starch.

Then soak the rice in enough water for 30 mins.

Boil 4 cups of water in a pan or pot.

Drain the rice and then add it to the boiling water.

Add all the whole spices - mace, cardamoms, cinnamon, cloves and tejpatta.

Season with salt and cook the rice till the grains are 3/4th cooked. Drain and keep the rice aside.

Once all the steam has gone from the rice, cover the rice.

chopping jackfruit

Now apply oil on your palms, knife and chopping board.

Chop the jackfruit and remove the seeds.

Whilst chopping, keep on adding the chopped jackfruit in a pan or a large bowl of water so that they don't darken.

If using chopped jackfruit already brought from outside, then rinse them in water.

The seeds can be added to vegetable dishes or in sambar or stir fries.

preparing jackfruit gravy for biryani

Heat ghee in a dutch oven or a pot.

Add all the whole spices - mace, stone flower, cinnamon, cloves, caraway seeds, cardamoms. Saute for some seconds till fragrant.

Add the sliced onions and fry them till they begin to get caramelized or golden.

When the onions begin to get golden, remove half of the onions and drain them on paper towels.

Add ginger, garlic and green chili paste. Saute for a few seconds till the raw aroma goes away.

Then add the tomatoes, mint leaves and coriander leaves. Saute for 1 to 2 mins.

Add both the spice powders - red chili powder and turmeric powder

Add the chopped jackfruit. Stir and saute for 7 to 8 mins. Then add the beaten yogurt.

Stir and add water. Add salt and cover the pot with its lid.

Simmer the gravy till the jackfruit is cooked and tender.

If the water dries up while cooking, then you can add some water.

Also soak saffron in warm milk and keep aside.

<u>assembling the kathal biryani</u>

In the same dutch oven or pot, on top of the jackfruit gravy, add half of the fried onions.

Spread a second layer of rice. Add all the rice in this layer.

If you want you can make 4 layers. Then you will have to make these layers in another pan or pot.

Sprinkle the saffron flavored milk along with the saffron threads, rose water or kewra water on the rice. Also dot with ghee.

<u>cooking kathal ki biryani</u>

If dum cooking on stove top - heat a tava or griddle. When the tava becomes hot, lower the flame. Place a moist kitchen napkin or towel on the pot covering it. Then place the lid tightly. The moist napkin or towel should not touch the biryani. Keep the pot on the tava and dum cook for 25 to 30 mins on a low flame.

If baking in the oven - cover the lid of the dutch oven tightly. Preheat the oven to 180 degrees c. Place the dutch oven in the oven and bake for 20 to 25 mins.

Once done, allow the jackfruit biryani to stand for 7 to 8 mins. Later serve the kathal biryani with raita, pickle and papad.

Cabbage Rice

This cabbage rice is Indian style fried rice made with cabbage, onions, tomatoes and spices.

Prep Time   :   40 mins

Cook Time   :   20 mins

Total Time   :   1 hr

Cuisine   :   Indian

Servings   :   3 to 4

<u>Ingredients</u>

<u>for cooking rice</u>

200 grams basmati rice or 1 cup heaped basmati rice - rinsed and soaked in water for 30 minutes

1.5 cups water for pressure cooking rice

¼ teaspoon salt as required

<u>other ingredients</u>

2 to 2.5 tablespoon oil

1 teaspoon cumin seeds

1 inch cinnamon

2 green cardamoms

2 cloves

1 small to medium tej patta (indian bay leaf)

1 medium onion chopped or 1/3 cup chopped onion

1 medium tomato chopped or 1/3 cup chopped tomatoes

½ inch ginger + 4 medium garlic + 1 or 2 green chilies - crushed to a paste in mortar-pestle

250 grams cabbage or 3 cups of shredded cabbage or half of a medium cabbage - shredded

¼ teaspoon turmeric powder (ground turmeric)

¼ teaspoon red chili powder

¼ teaspoon Garam Masala Powder

½ teaspoon coriander powder (ground coriander)

salt as required

some chopped coriander leaves (cilantro leaves) or mint leaves for garnishing

Instructions

cooking rice

Pick and rinse 1 cup (200 grams) basmati rice in running water till the water runs clear of starch. Soak the rice in enough water for 30 minutes. Later drain the rice and keep aside.

Add the rice in a pressure cooker. Also add 1.5 cups water and 1/4 tsp salt.

Pressure cook the rice for 2 to 3 whistles or for 9 to 10 minutes on a medium flame.

When the pressure comes down on its own, open the lid and fluff the rice with a fork. Keep aside and let the rice become warm or cool down at room temperature.

<u>preparation for cabbage rice</u>

When the rice is cooking, shred or grate 250 grams cabbage. You can also chop the cabbage. 250 grams cabbage gives about 3 cups of shredded cabbage. Keep aside.

Also crush 1/2 inch ginger + 4 medium garlic + 1 or 2 green chilies, in a mortar-pestle. Chop one medium onion as well as one medium tomato. Keep aside.

Before shredding the cabbage, peel and remove the top skin from the cabbage. Rinse and then halve or quarter the cabbage and blanch in hot water for about 5 minutes.

<u>making cabbage rice</u>

Heat 2 to 2.5 tbsp oil in a frying pan or wok. On a low to medium flame, add the whole spices - 1 tsp cumin seeds, 1 inch cinnamon, 2 green cardamoms, 2 cloves and 1 small to medium tej patta. Saute the spices till they splutter and become fragrant.

Then add 1/3 cup chopped onions.

On a medium flame, stir and saute the onions till translucent.

Next add crushed 1/2 inch ginger + 4 medium garlic + 1 or 2 green chilies. You can crush in a mortar-pestle.

Saute till the raw aroma of ginger and garlic goes away.

Next add 1/3 cup chopped tomatoes. stir well.

Then add 1/4 tsp turmeric powder, 1/4 tsp red chili powder, 1/4 tsp garam masala powder and 1/2 tsp coriander powder.

On a medium flame, stir and saute the whole masala till the tomatoes soften and become pulpy. You should also see oil releasing from the sides.

Now add the shredded cabbage. At this step, if you want then you can also add grated carrot, green peas and chopped potato cubes.

Mix the cabbage very well with the rest of the masala.

Season with salt as per taste.

Stir fry the cabbage on a medium flame and cook them till they turn translucent.

Then add the cooked rice.

Gently mix the rice with the cabbage mixture. You can also add the rice in parts and mix.

Saute the cabbage fried rice for 2 to 3 minutes more after mixing.

Garnish with coriander leaves or mint leaves.

Serve cabbage rice hot with a simple dal or raita or you can also have it plain.

Pineapple Fried Rice

Pineapple fried rice is a simple & delicious lightly spiced fried rice made with fresh pineapple.

Prep Time   : 20 mins

Cook Time   : 20 mins

Total Time   : 40 mins

Cuisine   : Indo Chinese, World

Servings   : 3 to 4

<u>Ingredients</u>

<u>for cooking rice</u>

200 grams basmati rice or 1 cup basmati rice or long grained rice - rinsed and then soaked in 1 cup water for 20 minutes.

½ teaspoon salt

½ teaspoon oil

4 to 4.5 cups water for cooking rice

other ingredients

1 cup chopped pineapple cubes

1 to 2 green chilies or fresh red chilies - chopped or sliced

1 medium onion finely chopped or ⅓ cup finely chopped onion (spring onions can also be used instead of onions)

2 to 3 garlic, finely chopped or ½ teaspoon finely chopped garlic

½ teaspoon finely chopped celery (optional)

½ teaspoon crushed black pepper or add as per taste

1 tablespoon naturally fermented soy sauce - add as required

½ tablespoon red chili sauce or sriracha sauce - add more as per taste

¼ cup cashews

2 tablespoon oil

salt as required

2 to 3 tablespoon chopped coriander leaves or 1 to 2 tablespoon chopped parsley leaves

Instructions

cooking rice

Rinse rice very well till the water runs clear of starch. Soak rice in water for 20 mins. Drain and keep aside.

In a pot, bring to a boil 4 to 4.5 cups of water with 1/2 tsp salt and 1/2 tsp oil.

Add the soaked and drained rice to the hot water.

On a low to medium flame cook the rice without the lid.

When the rice becomes al dente or just cooked, remove the pot from fire and drain the rice.

While straining, you can also gently rinse the rice in water so that they stop cooking and don't stick to each other. You can also fluff the rice with a fork and keep aside. Cover the rice and keep aside till the rice cools completely.

making pineapple fried rice

When the rice is soaking, prep the other ingredients. Peel and chop the pineapple in small cubes. Also chop the other ingredients like onion, green chilies & garlic.

Heat 2 tbsp oil in a kadai or wok. Add 1/3 cup finely chopped onions. Spring onions can also be used instead of onions.

On a low to medium flame, saute for a minute.

Add 1 to 2 green chilies or red chilies (chopped or sliced), ½ tsp finely chopped garlic and ½ tsp finely chopped celery (optional). Stir and saute for a few seconds.

Then add ¼ cup cashews.

Saute for 3 to 4 minutes till the cashews become a light golden or golden.

Add the pineapple cubes.

Stir and saute the pineapple cubes for 4 to 5 minutes till the moisture dries up. You can also saute the pineapple cubes till they caramelize.

Add freshly crushed black pepper. Stir very well.

Add 1 tbsp naturally fermented soy sauce. You can add soy sauce as per taste preferences. Mix well.

Add ½ tbsp red chili sauce or sriracha sauce. You can add more or less as per your taste.

Mix the sauces very well with the rest of the ingredients.

Add the cooked rice. Season with salt.

Stir gently and mix the rice very well with the rest of the ingredients. Saute for 2 to 3 minutes with occasional stirrings.

Lastly add 3 tbsp chopped coriander leaves. You can also add 2 tbsp parsley leaves instead of coriander leaves. Stir well.

Serve pineapple fried rice plain or with stir fried veggies.

<u>Notes</u>

Substitutions:Pineapple - apple or pearCashews - chopped almonds, walnuts, pistachios, pine nutsBlack pepper - white pepper powder.

Parsi Brown Rice

Aromatic, golden with a faint sweet tinge is this rice dish made with basmati rice, whole spices, sugar and onions

Prep Time   :   30 mins

Cook Time   :   20 mins

Total Time   :   50 mins

Cuisine   :   Paris

Servings   :   3 to 4

<u>*Ingredients*</u>

1 cup basmati rice

1 inch cinnamon

2 to 3 cloves

2 to 3 green cardamoms

2 to 3 whole black peppercorns

1 medium sized onion, thinly sliced

½ to 1 teaspoon regular sugar or ½ to 1 teaspoon organic unrefined cane sugar

1 tablespoon oil or ghee (clarified butter)

2.5 to 3 cups water

salt as required

Instructions

Soak the basmati rice in enough water for 30 mins. After 30 mins, drain the rice and keep aside.

Heat oil or ghee in a thick bottomed pot. Add the cinnamon, cardamom, cloves and black pepper. Fry till they get fragrant.

Add the sliced onions. Stir and fry the onions till they get translucent and are softened.

Now add sugar and stir. Continue frying the onions till they caramelize or get browned.

The sugar will also caramelize. Keep on stirring in between to ensure even browning.

When the onions have got browned, quickly remove some onions for garnishing. They will have a sweet taste and will be a little sticky due to the caramelization of sugar.

Add the rice and gently stir. Pour 4 cups of water. Add salt and stir.

Cover tightly and let the rice cook till done and all the water is absorbed.

Check once or twice when the rice is cooking.

If the water is all absorbed and the rice is not cooked completely, then add a few tbsps of water.

Don't stir as you don't want to break the rice grains. Cover and cook the rice for 2-3 minutes more.

Serve parsi brown rice garnished with the fried onions with veg dhansak, patio or parsi dal.

Vangi Bath (Brinjal Rice)

Vangi bath is a delicious recipe of brinjal rice from Karnataka cuisine. This Vangi bath recipe makes use of vangi bath masala powder and tamarind pulp as two of the main ingredients.

Prep Time   :   30 mins

Cook Time   :   20 mins

Total Time   :   50 mins

Cuisine   :   Karnataka

Servings   :   2

Ingredients

for cooking rice

225 grams sona masuri rice or 1 heaped cup of rice

¼ teaspoon salt

2 cups water

for preparing tamarind pulp

½ tablespoon tightly packed tamarind

¼ cup hot water

other ingredients

2 tablespoons peanut oil - can also use sesame oil or sunflower oil

½ teaspoon mustard seeds

½ teaspoon urad dal

2 tablespoons roasted peanuts or cashews

1 sprig curry leaves or 10 to 12 curry leaves

⅛ teaspoon asafoetida (hing)

1 to 2 dry red chilies

200 grams small to medium sized green or purple brinjal (baingan or vangi or egg plant) - cut in long pieces and soaked in salted water for 15 to 20 minutes

¼ teaspoon turmeric powder

2 to 2.5 tablespoons vangi bath masala powder

salt as per taste

2 tablespoon fresh grated coconut, optional

¼ to ½ teaspoon jaggery powder

2 to 3 tablespoons chopped coriander leaves - optional

Instructions

preparation

First soak 1 heaped cup of rice in water for 30 minutes. Use any regular rice. I used sona masuri rice.

Then pressure cook the rice with 2 cups of water, ¼ teaspoon salt for 3 to 4 whistles on a medium flame or for 11 to 12 minutes. You can also cook the rice in a pot. If cooking in a pot, then you may need to add more water.

Soak ½ tablespoon tightly packed tamarind in ¼ cup hot water for 20 to 30 minutes.

Later squeeze the soaked tamarind in the water to get the tamarind pulp. Strain and keep aside.

When the pressure settles down on its own, open the cooker's lid and fluff the rice.

You can allow the rice to cool in the cooker itself or spread rice on a large plate/thali or tray. Allow the cooked rice grains to become warm or cool down. Cover and keep so that the rice grains do not dry out.

When the rice is cooking, rinse the brinjals. Remove the crowns of the brinjals and slice them vertically in 4 long pieces. As soon as you chop them, place them in a bowl containing water to which some salt has been added.

Do make sure that there is sufficient water covering the brinjals. Allow them to be in the salted water for 15 to 20 minutes.

making vangi bath

Heat 2 tablespoons peanut oil (can also use sesame oil or sunflower oil) in a pan or kadai.

Add ½ teaspoon mustard seeds.

Once the mustard seeds begin to crackle, then add ½ teaspoon urad dal.

Next add 2 tablespoons roasted peanuts or cashews.

Saute till the urad dal becomes golden.

Then add 1 to 2 dry red chilies, 1 sprig curry leaves or 10 to 12 curry leaves and ⅛ teaspoon asafoetida (about 2 pinches of asafoetida).

Add the brinjals. Just remove the brinjals from the salted water and add in the pan. Be careful as the mixture sputters when adding brinjals.

Mix them with the rest of the tempering mixture.

Add ¼ teaspoon turmeric powder. Also add salt as per taste.

Mix the turmeric powder and salt very well.

Cover the pan with a lid and let the brinjals get half-cooked. Do check at intervals. While cooking, if the brinjals start sticking to the pan then add some water. Then cover and cook.

Half cook the brinjals.

Once they are half done, then add the tamarind pulp.

Then add 2 to 2.5 tablespoons vangi bath masala powder.

Mix very well and continue to cook without the lid. If the masala along with brinjals start sticking to the pan, then add ¼ cup water and continue to cook.

Once the brinjals are cooked well, add 2 tablespoons grated coconut and ¼ to ½ teaspoon jaggery powder.

Mix again very well. The brinjal masala is thick. But for some moisture you can have a semi gravy consistency in the brinjal masala.

Keep the pan down and add rice in two to three parts. Mix gently.

Add the next portion of rice and then mix well.

Mix gently but very well so that everything is mixed evenly.

Serve vangi bath with raita, papads or chips.

Zarda Recipe

Zarda recipe of meethe chawal or zarda pulao is a fragrant sweet pulao made with rice, dry fruits and saffron.

Prep Time   :   30 mins

Cook Time   :   20 mins

Total Time   :   50 mins

Cuisine   :   North Indian

Servings   :   3

Ingredients

<u>for cooking rice</u>

½ cup basmati rice

enough water for soaking rice

5 to 6 cloves

⅛ teaspoon saffron or 3 to 4 pinches saffron (kesar)

1 cup water for pressure cooking rice

other ingredients

3 tablespoons ghee (clarified butter)

¾ teaspoon green cardamom powder

½ cup sugar

8 almonds - chopped or sliced

8 cashews - chopped or sliced

8 pistachios - chopped or sliced

10 to 12 raisins or add as required

Instructions

pressure cooking rice

Rinse ½ cup basmati rice very well in water till the water runs clear of starch. Then soak basmati rice for 30 minutes in enough water. After 30 minutes drain all the water and keep rice aside.

In a 2 litre pressure cooker, pour 1 cup water.

Add ⅛ teaspoon saffron strands (3 to 4 pinches).

With a spoon stir, so that the saffron strands mix with water.

Then add ½ cup rice and 5 to 6 cloves. You can even add 7 to 9 cloves if you want.

Pressure cook for 2 whistles or for about 6 to 7 minutes on medium flame.

Once the pressure settles down, then open the lid and check the rice if it's cooked. The rice just needs to be cooked. Gently fluff the rice.

<u>making zarda</u>

In a heavy kadai or pan, add 3 tablespoons ghee.

With a spoon or spatula spread ghee on all sides of the pan. This is done so that the rice grains do not stick to the pan when cooking.

Add the cooked rice in the pan.

Add ½ cup sugar.

Sprinkle ¾ teaspoon cardamom powder. You can also add 1 teaspoon cardamom powder for a pronounced cardamom aroma.

Mix well but gently, so that the sugar gets mixed evenly with cooked rice grains.

On a low flame or low heat, cook the pulao mixture. You will see the sugar melting and some liquid consistency in pulao.

Stir the zarda pulao mixture occasionally.

Cook till the sugar solution dries up. After cooking, if in case the rice grains feel hard or dense, then cover the pan with a damp cloth or cotton napkin. Cover with a lid and cook pulao for 20 to 30 seconds.

Once there is no liquid consistency, then add 8 pistachios (sliced), 8 almonds (sliced) and 8 cashews (sliced). Mix well and switch off the flame. If adding raisins, then you can add at this step.

Serve zarda rice hot or warm. Alternatively you can spread zarda on a large plate and then serve. Garnish zarda pulao with some cashews, raisins, almonds and pistachios while serving.

<u>Notes</u>

The recipe can be doubled or tripled.

You can use a neutral flavored oil instead of ghee.

Add dry fruits of your choice.

If you want you can add a bit of orange or yellow natural color extract.

Potato Dum Biryani

Layered and dum cooked biryani made from baby potatoes.

Prep Time   :   30 mins

Cook Time   :   30 mins

Total Time   :   1 hr

Cuisine   :   Hyderabadi, South Indian

Servings   :   4

<u>*Ingredients*</u>

<u>for cooking rice</u>

1.5 cups basmati rice or 300 grams basmati rice

5 cups water for cooking rice

1 teaspoon salt or add as required

1 small to medium tej patta (indian bay leaf)

2 cloves

2 green cardamoms

1 inch cinnamon

3 to 4 strands of mace

<u>for ground paste</u>

2 green chillies

¼ cup chopped coriander leaves

2 tablespoons chopped mint leaves

½ inch ginger - roughly chopped

5 small to medium garlic - roughly chopped

⅓ cup Curd (yogurt)

<u>for frying</u>

3 tablespoons ghee (clarified butter)

250 grams baby potatoes or 12 to 15 baby potatoes

15 cashews

½ tablespoon raisins

<u>for biryani gravy</u>

1 inch cinnamon

1 small to medium tejpatta (indian bay leaf)

3 green cardamoms

1 black cardamom

2 cloves

125 grams onions or 2 medium onions or 1 cup tightly packed thinly sliced onions

75 grams tomatoes or 1 medium tomato or 1/2 cup chopped tomatoes

½ teaspoon turmeric powder

½ teaspoon red chilli powder

1 teaspoon coriander powder

1 teaspoon biryani masala powder or garam masala powder

½ cup water

<u>**for layering**</u>

1 pinch of saffron

3 tablespoons warm water

2 teaspoons rose water or kewra water

Instructions

cooking rice

Rinse 1.5 cups basmati rice (300 grams) very well in water till the water runs clear of starch. Soak rice grains in enough water for 30 minutes.

On a medium to high flame, bring to boil 5 cups water, 1 teaspoon salt, 1 small to medium tej patta, 2 cloves, 2 green cardamoms, 1 inch cinnamon, 3 to 4 strands of mace.

When the water comes to boil, add the rice. Do not reduce the flame and cook the rice.

Cook rice till its ¾th done or 75% cooked. Check the doneness by biting a few grains of rice. You should get a slight bite in the rice.

Then drain the rice in a colander. If you want you can even rinse the cooked rice with fresh water. Keep aside.

preparation to make gravy for biryani

In a chutney grinder jar or small grinder, take 2 green chillies, ¼ cup chopped coriander leaves, 2 tablespoons chopped mint leaves, ½ inch ginger (roughly chopped), 5 small to medium garlic (roughly chopped).

Add ⅓ cup fresh curd (yogurt or dahi).

Grind to smooth or a semi fine paste. Keep aside.

Heat 3 tablespoons ghee (clarified butter) in a pan.

When the ghee becomes hot, add peeled baby potatoes (250 grams or 12 to 15 baby potatoes). If the potatoes are large, then halve or quarter them and then add.

Fry the potatoes on medium flame till they are 90% cooked or almost cooked.

Remove with a slotted spoon and place the potatoes on kitchen paper towels.

Next add 15 cashews (kaju) in the pan and fry till the cashews become golden. Remove and keep aside.

Next add ½ tablespoon raisins (kishmish) and fry till they become plump. remove and keep aside.

In the same pan now add the following spices - 1 inch cinnamon, 3 green cardamoms, 2 cloves, 1 black cardamom and 1 small to medium tejpatta. The oil will be hot, so the spices will crackle as soon as you add them.

Quickly add 1 cup tightly packed thinly sliced onions.

Begin to saute the onions on low to medium flame stirring often till they turn golden or caramelize.

Then quickly remove half of the fried onions from the pan.

Keep the fried onions aside along with remaining fried ingredients.

<u>making gravy for biryani</u>

Now add ½ cup chopped tomatoes

Sauté the tomatoes till they turn mushy.

Keep the flame to a low and add ½ teaspoon turmeric powder, ½ teaspoon red chilli powder, 1 teaspoon coriander powder and 1 teaspoon biryani masala powder or garam masala powder. Mix very well.

Then add the ground paste. mix very well and saute the masala till you see oil releasing from the sides.

Now add ½ cup water. season with salt as per taste. Mix very well.

Add half of the fried potatoes and mix again.

Simmer the gravy on a medium flame for 8 to 9 minutes or till the gravy thickens a bit. Keep aside.

<u>assembling and layering aloo dum biryani</u>

When the gravy is cooking, soak 1 pinch of saffron (kesar) in 3 tablespoons of warm water. Keep aside.

Now take half of the gravy and layer it in a thick bottomed pan.

Layer half of the rice.

Next add some of the fried potatoes, cashews and raisins. layer with some of the fried onions.

Add half of the saffron dissolved water.

Repeat the gravy, rice, fried potatoes, onions, cashews and raisins layer. Add the remaining saffron soaked water. Also add 2 teaspoons of rose water or kewra water.

dum cooking potato biryani

Seal the pan with aluminium foil.

Cover the pan with its lid and place it on a preheated tava or griddle. Preheat the tawa on a low to medium flame for 5 minutes before you place the pan.

Dum cook biryani on low flame or sim for 30 minutes.

If baking – preheat the oven to 180 degree celsius and then bake in a preheated oven for 25-30 minutes. Please remember to use an oven proof glass utensil like the pyrex bowl for baking in the oven. You will have to assemble the biryani as mentioned above in the ovenproof utensil. Cover with aluminum foil or the pyrex bowl lid and then bake.

Give a resting time of 5 to 7 minutes and check the biryani.

If you see a lot of gravy in the biryani, then cover and continue to dum cook. There should be no liquid or gravy at the bottom of the pan.

If there is some gravy, then seal again and continue to dum cook for some more minutes.

You can garnish with some mint or coriander leaves if you want. Serve the biryani with your favorite raita or salan.

Cauliflower Biryani

This Cauliflower biryani is a one-pot recipe of a dum cooked South Indian style biryani made with cauliflower florets, coconut, herbs and spices.

Prep Time   : 30 mins

Cook Time   : 30 mins

Total Time   : 1 hr

Cuisine   : South Indian

Servings   : 4

Ingredients

Blanching cauliflower (optional step)

3 cups cauliflower florets or 1 small to medium-sized cauliflower

hot water - as required for blanching cauliflower

½ teaspoon vinegar - optional

¼ teaspoon salt

Spices to be ground

1 inch cinnamon

3 cloves

3 green cardamoms

1 small piece of stone flower (dagad phool) - optional

2 to 3 strands of mace

½ teaspoon cumin seeds

½ teaspoon poppy seeds (khus khus) - optional

1 teaspoon coriander seeds

5 whole black peppers

½ teaspoon fennel seeds

3 tablespoons desiccated coconut or fresh coconut

2 green chilies - chopped or ½ tablespoon chopped - you can add more green chillies for a spicy biryani

1 inch ginger - chopped or ½ tablespoon chopped ginger

½ tablespoon chopped garlic or 4 to 5 medium-sized garlic cloves

2 tablespoon chopped coriander leaves (cilantro)

¼ cup water for grinding

<u>For soaking rice</u>

1.5 cups seeraga samba rice or 280 grams - can sub with basmati rice

water - as required for soaking rice

<u>Other ingredients</u>

3 tablespoons oil - any neutral tasting oil

½ cup thinly sliced onions or 1 medium-sized onion

5 to 6 curry leaves

1 cup finely chopped tomatoes or 2 medium-sized tomatoes

1 pinch of turmeric powder (ground turmeric)

1 medium potato or a fistful of green peas - both are optional

3 cups water

1 teaspoon lemon juice

salt as required

1 to 2 tablespoons coriander leaves (cilantro) - for garnish

Instructions

Soaking rice

Rinse 1.5 cups seeraga samba rice (280 grams) 3 to 4 times in water. Then soak rice grains for 30 minutes in enough water. After 30 minutes, drain the rice and keep aside.

Blanching cauliflower

Next rinse and then chop 1 small to medium cauliflower in medium sized florets. You will need about 3 cups of cauliflower florets. Take the florets in a bowl. Add hot boiling water till it covers the cauliflower florets. Also add ¼ teaspoon salt. Keep aside for 5 to 6 minutes.

Blanching the cauliflower is to get rid of the worms or insects. This step is optional. To get rid of the cauliflower aroma, you can add ½ teaspoon vinegar in the hot water and mix it well before adding gobi florets.

Preparing spice paste

Meanwhile prepare the spice paste or masala paste. Take all the whole spices mentioned above in the list 'spices to be ground' in a small grinder jar or chutney grinder jar.

Also add desiccated coconut, green chilies, ginger, garlic and coriander leaves.

Add ¼ cup water and grind to a smooth paste. Keep the spice paste aside.

Sautéing onions and tomatoes

Heat 3 tablespoons oil in a thick bottomed heavy pan or pot. Add ½ cup thinly sliced onions.

Begin to sauté onions on a low to medium flame till they turn golden.

Then add 5 to 6 curry leaves and 1 cup finely chopped tomatoes. Mix very well.

Cover the pan and cook the tomatoes for 4 to 5 minutes on a low flame, till they soften and become mushy. In between do check a couple of times and stir, so that the tomatoes do not stick to the bottom of the pan.

Then add the ground masala paste. mix and sauté for 1 to 2 minutes.

Then add a pinch of turmeric powder and mix again.

Adding cauliflower and rice

Now add the blanched cauliflower florets.

Mix the cauliflower florets with the rest of the masala.

Then add the rice and gently mix the rice grains with the rest of the ingredients.

Add 3 cups of water. next add 1 teaspoon lemon juice and salt as per taste.

Check the taste of the water and it should have a slight salty taste. Stir well.

Dum cooking cauliflower biryani

Seal the pan with an aluminium foil.

Now cover the pan with its lid. You can even directly keep the lid on the pan without using the foil. Since this lid has a vent on it, I have sealed the pan with the foil.

Dum cook the biryani for 18 to 20 minutes on a low flame or sim. Do use a thick bottomed heavy pan or else the base can get browned or burnt. If doubtful, then keep the pan on a hot heavy tawa (griddle) which is placed on the burner and cook on a low flame.

Give a standing time of 6 to 8 minutes. Then open the lid. Gently fluff the biryani and serve hot.

Garnish with coriander leaves while serving gobi biryani. Serve any raita or salad of your choice with this cauliflower biryani.

Notes

Instead of seeraga samba rice, you can use other Indian varieties of rice like basmati rice or sona masuri rice or amber mohur rice (mango blossom rice) or sella basmati rice (parboiled basmati rice).

Add more green chilies for a spicy taste in the biryani.

Do use a thick bottomed heavy and deep pan or pot, so that the rice does not get burnt while dum cooking.

Blanching cauliflower is an optional step and you can skip it if there are no insects or worms in it.

Skip poppy seeds and stone flowers if you do not have them.

If you want to include more veggies then you can consider adding green peas, potatoes and carrots. You can add them in the step when you add the cauliflower.

Since this is a complexly flavored biryani, you will have to use the method of approximation (or andaaz in Hindi) when doubling the recipe.

Vermicelli Biryani

Vermicelli biryani is a delicious biryani variety made with seviyan.

Prep Time   :   20 mins

Cook Time :   40 mins

Total Time   :   1 hr

Cuisine   :   Rajasthani

Servings   :   3

<u>Ingredients</u>

<u>for bouquet garni or spices potli</u>

2 teaspoons coriander seeds

½ teaspoon cumin seeds

½ teaspoon fennel seeds

1 inch ginger, crushed

4 to 5 garlic, crushed

1 tej patta (indian bay leaf)

5 to 6 whole black peppercorns

1 inch cinnamon

1 black cardamom - lightly crushed

2 green cardamom - lightly crushed

2 cloves - lightly crushed

ingredients for yakhni or stock

½ cup heaped chopped carrots

½ cup heaped chopped potatoes

¼ cup chopped french beans

⅓ cup green peas, fresh or frozen

1 teaspoon salt or add as required

2 cups water or add as required

for roasting vermicelli

½ tablespoon ghee (clarified butter)

1 cup vermicelli - 75 grams (semiya or seviyan)

for frying onions

1.5 tablespoons ghee

1 large onion - thinly sliced or 1 cup thinly sliced onions

other ingredient

1 teaspoon kewra water or rose water - optional

Instructions

making bouquet garni or spices potli

In a muslin or cotton kitchen napkin, take all the spices and herbs mentioned above in the list 'for bouquet garni or spices potli'.

Take the ends of the muslin and secure or tie it like a potli (small bundle). Keep aside.

making yakhni or stock

Rinse, peel and chop the veggies. Then add them in the pressure cooker.

Then add 1 teaspoon salt or add as required.

Add 2 cups of water. Depending on the type of seviyan used, you can add 2 to 2.25 cups of water. If using a pan to make yakhni, then add 2.5 cups of water.

Place the prepared spice bag (potli).

Pressure cook for 1 to 2 whistles or 9 to 10 minutes on medium flame.

When the pressure settles down on its own, open the lid and check if the veggies are done. Let the yakhni stock become warm.

Squeeze the spice bag to extract more of the spice flavors. Remove it from the yakhni stock. Check the taste of the stock and add more salt if required. The yakhni should have a slightly salty taste. Then cover and keep the mixed vegetable yakhni aside.

roasting semiya

Meanwhile in another pan heat ½ tablespoon ghee.

Keep the flame to low or medium-low. Add broken vermicelli.

Mix the vermicelli strands with the ghee and begin to roast them.

Roast stirring continuously so that semiya strands get evenly cooked and roasted till light golden or golden. Remove in a pan and keep aside.

In the same pan, now heat 1.5 tablespoons ghee. add 1 cup thinly sliced onions.

Begin to sauté onions on a medium-low flame.

Continue to sauté them stirring often till they turn golden and caramelized. Remove the pan from the stove top and keep aside.

assembling and layering semiya biryani

First add the roasted seviyan in the stock.

With a spoon distribute the seviyan evenly all over.

Reserve 1 to 2 tablespoons of the fried onions and sprinkle remaining fried onions all over. At this step you can also add 1 teaspoon of rose water or kewra water. If using rose essence or kewra essence, then just add about 2 to 3 drops.

Cover the cooker with a moist cotton napkin or cotton kitchen towel.

Place a lid. On top of a lid place a heavy weight like a mortar-pestle.

Heat a tawa (or griddle) on a medium flame for 5 minutes. Then lower the flame. Keep the entire cooker set up on the tawa. Dum cook seviyan biryani on low flame for 20 to 25 minutes.

After switching off the flame, allow a standing time for 4 to 5 minutes. Then remove the lid.

Check the biryani at the bottom of the cooker and there should be no water. All the water should be absorbed. If there is water, then continue to dum cook for some more minutes.

Mix gently and serve hot with raita or tomato shorba.

www.ingramcontent.com/pod-product-compliance
Lightning Source LLC
Chambersburg PA
CBHW021359150726
47989CB00005B/2312